PRAISE FOR
Dr. Washington's *Driven to Succeed*

"Washington's compelling memoir mixes the history of the civil rights movement with her superb storytelling woven around her life struggles and leaves the reader impressed and inspired by her faith in God."

– Diann Dawson, President, Potomac Valley Section, National Council of Negro Women, Inc. (NCNW)

"Dr. Hattie Washington's story displays American determination at its best. Although she started with humble beginnings in rural Virginia, she used education as a stepping stone to achieve high levels of excellence. Her accomplishments are a model for young men and women everywhere."

– Dr. Stephanie E. Myers, National Co-Chair, Black Women for Positive Change

"Washington's divine interventions are compelling and stimulate the reader to reflect personally on their life from a positive standpoint."

–Jacquelyn Gaines, National Speaker, Business Executive, and Bestselling author of *The Yellow Suit: A Guide for Women in Leadership*

DRIVEN
TO
SUCCEED

DRIVEN TO SUCCEED

~ An Inspirational Memoir of Lessons Learned
Through Faith, Family and Favor ~

Dr. Hattie N. Washington

WASHINGTON
PUBLISHING™
ENTERPRISES
Hanover • Jacksonville • Virginia Beach • Norfolk

DRIVEN TO SUCCEED. An Inspirational Memoir of Lessons Learned Through Faith, Family and Favor.

Copyright © 2019 by Dr. Hattie N. Washington. All rights reserved. Printed in the United States of America. No part of this book may be used or reproduced in any manner whatsoever without written permission, except in the case of brief quotations, poems, and anecdotes embodied in critical articles and reviews if credit is given to the author. Published by Washington Publishing Enterprises, 7789 Arundel Mills Blvd, #224, Hanover, Maryland 21076, USA.

The author and President/CEO of Washington Publishing Enterprises can be available for your live events: keynote speeches, workshops, training, consultant, book clubs, book signings, etc. For more information or to book an event with the author, visit our website at: www.drhnwashington.com or email the author at drhattie@washingtonpublishingenterprises.com.

For information about special discounts for bulk purchases, please contact call Washington Publishing Enterprises Special Sales at 443-804-6545 or the distributer at https://www.ingramcontent.com/retailers/ordering –1-855-997-7275 (US) or +44(0)808 164 8277 (INTL).

Cover and logo designed by Bruce Smallwood of Mt. Vernon Marketing.

Cover photographs by Kea Taylor of Imagine Photography.

Cover photographs of Former President Bill Clinton, Dr. Dorothy Height, and Actress Victoria Rowell courtesy of the author.

All photographs courtesy of the author except where otherwise indicated.

Library of Congress Number: 2019905485

Library of Congress Cataloging-in-Publication Data
Washington, Dr. Hattie N.
Driven To Succeed: An Inspirational Memoir of Lessons Learned
Through Faith, Family and Favor/Dr. Hattie Washington p. cm

Paperback: ISBN: 13: 978-1-950707-03-4
                   10: 1-950707-03-2

Hardcopy: ISBN: 13: 978-1-950707-04-1
                   10: 1-950707-04-01

E-Book: ISBN: 13: 978-1-950707-05-8
                   10: 1-950707-05-9

Printed in the United States of America

10 9 8 7 6 5 4 3 2 1

Publisher's Note

The scanning, uploading, distribution of this book via the Internet or via any other means without the permission of the publisher/author is illegal and punishable by law. Please purchase only authorized electronic editions and do not participate in or encourage electronic piracy of copyrightable materials. Your support of the author's rights is appreciated.

Author's Note

I have tried to recreate events, locales and conversations from my memories of them. In order to maintain their anonymity in some instances, I have changed the names of individual and places. I may have changed some identifying characteristics and details such as physical properties, occupations and places of residence.

"There wasn't any fear. I just felt this is your moment, SEIZE IT!"

– BARBARA JOHNS

I Wish to Dedicate My Book To

my 90-year-old aunt, Hattie Kindred Fenner, the matriarch of the family and after whom I was named
(Has deceased since the initial publication of this book in 2015)

Acknowledgments

I wish to personally thank the following people for their contributions and knowledge helping in creating this book: My inspiring cousin, Lorenzo Goganious, the patriarch of the family and more like a brother, who gave me the idea and the encouragement to write my memoir.

Thank you to my two daughters, Charrell Washington-Thomas, MD, and Cheryl Washington, Esq., whom I am immensely proud and feel incredibly blessed to have had the sheer joy of rearing these two extraordinary young ladies; my awesome adopted Son, Wayne Saunders; my favorite son-in-law, Sean Thomas; and my amazing granddaughters, Cameron and Reagan Thomas. Thank you all for reading my book and encouraging me to finish my memoir.

Thank you to my foster young men over the years. You have inspired me more than you will ever know to write my story.

To my supporters who took the time to read my book and give me valuable feedback: Julie Haskins-Turner, Marilyn Massey-Ball, Stephanie Parrish, Dr. Lucille Ellis, Cheryl Washington, Charrell W. Thomas, Sean Thomas, Bettie Goganious, Vivian Malloy, Eunita Winkey, Diane Battle, Dr. Melody Jackson, Laura Goodman, Wayne Saunders, Charlene Weston, Diann Dawson and Brenita Young of NCNW–PVS, Audrey Meredith, Chair, Aunt Hattie's Place Board of Directors; Reverend Lisa Holloway of Circle Fellowship Church, Kathy Hambrecht, Jon Winter, Mary Johnson and Pamela Hendershot of Hope House of Maryland, and Emily Vaias of Linowes & Blocher.

Much gratitude and appreciation to Bruce Smallwood of Mt. Vernon Marketing for his personable and invaluable expertise during the whole self-publishing process—from designing my logo for my new publishing company, designing the front and back book covers, as well as formatting the book. I also thank several of my fellow authors who provided great advice, reviews, resources and services available to authors and publishers. You made the whole process a spiritual and emotional learning experience.

Lastly, but in no means least, my Thank You, God Prayer: I Thank God for His Almighty power and His Favor of me to give me the necessary strength, inspiration, wisdom, and wit to pen this memoir to give appreciation, recognition, and exhortation to His Name. May God richly bless each person who reads this book and who endeavors to "give back" to the community and make a difference in the world. Amen.

"There is no greater agony than bearing an untold story inside you."

– MAYA ANGELOU, *I Know Why the Caged Bird Sings*

Table of Contents

Acknowledgements xiii
Introduction. xix

~PART ONE~
FAITH AND FAMILY

CHAPTER 1: First Wave of the Baby Boomers: Aiming to Make a Difference 3
CHAPTER 2: Where It All Began 21
CHAPTER 3: Massive Resistance in a Small Town: School Closings 29
CHAPTER 4: Going Back Home 61
CHAPTER 5: Raising the Bar: Rearing My Daughters to Become Professional Women 93
CHAPTER 6: The Dark Secret 109

~PART TWO~
FAITH AND FAVOR

CHAPTER 7: Aunt Hattie's Place 129
CHAPTER 8: "IF I Grow Up" 139
CHAPTER 9: Mentor Mothers and Fathers. 153
CHAPTER 10: Miracles: Divine Intervention 191
CHAPTER 11: Lessons Learned 201

Thank-You Letters from My Daughters and Son 211
Resources 217
Special Recognition from the Author. 223

Introduction

"I can do all things through Christ who strengthens me."
– PHILIPPIANS 4:13 (KJV)

One day, a 16-year-old girl decided she had had enough of the terrible conditions of her high school, a school built to house 180 students, but held 450 students. To pacify the students and the parents, rather than building a new larger high school, the county built long temporary buildings that looked like chicken coops to house the overflow of black students. The 16-year-old girl and most of her fellow students walked out of their high school and made history.

The date was April 23, 1951, when the average gas price was 10 cents per gallon. The young student's name was Barbara Johns, niece of civil rights pioneer Reverend Vernon Johns. The high school was R. R. Moton High School. Not only did Barbara Johns organize the two-week strike, she and her uncle called the NAACP, which included noted lawyers, Thurgood Marshall, who ultimately became the first African-American United States Supreme Court Justice, and Oliver W. Hill, to help them in their fight for better facilities. The thing that was so significant about the strike at R. R. Moton High School was that it was the catalyst that eventually led to the historic landmark case, *Brown v. Board of Education.*

I was too young when the strike occurred; however, like Barbara Johns and the other prominent figures I named, I, too, experienced racism, even after the separate but equal policies were struck down by the U.S. Supreme Court. And, like Barbara Johns, I lived in Prince Edward County, Virginia, during my early childhood years, right in the era of the civil rights movement, a time when African-American people weren't given the same respect and opportunities as white people. As Barbara Johns succinctly put it, "It was like reaching for the moon."

In the summer of 1959, at the age of thirteen, I learned that I would be leaving the only family I had known. I would be heading to another city for education purposes, because the county in which I lived chose to close the schools rather than desegregate them. Though I was devastated about my plight, I was driven to execute a survival action plan for my life and made every effort to follow that plan to accomplish the things that I wanted and was expected to accomplish. When I think back to the early part of my life, I realize how fortunate I was to have had a father who loved me unconditionally and who was the ultimate role model. Although we were in a time of uncertainty, the era of segregation and desegregation, I was taught by my father values and morals that I still live by to this day.

My father taught me, "If you don't stand for something, you'll fall for anything"; "We have got to be twice as qualified just to get one-half of an opportunity"; "When given the opportunity, work twice as hard to prove that you are qualified, and not just a token— not only for yourself personally, but also for your family and your race"; "It's nice to be important, but it's more important to be nice"; and many other pearls of wisdom. I've passed along these same principles and morals to my daughters, foster sons, and my granddaughters.

My first cousin, Lorenzo Goganious, whom I consider more a brother than a cousin, called at 6:30 AM one day in February 2014. He told me that he had a vision of me writing a book to share my parental principles of rearing two daughters, one a medical doctor and the other one a lawyer, and how I helped my foster boys and other students over the years to believe and achieve.

It was a vision indeed because on the same day, that evening, I received another confirmation from my good friendMarilyn Massey-Ball that I should write a book. While eating dinner, we talked about the book idea over fried flounder and two slices of Smith Island nine-layer, pineapple-coconut cake (a must-splurge), at the renowned Crisfield Restaurant in Silver Spring, Maryland.

After both affirmations and a previous spiritual revelation, I knew then that it was time to write my book, as I had been putting it off, to make a difference in the lives of deserving foster boys. I started jotting down thoughts and events that took place in my life that propelled me and inspired me day by day. Now some twenty years later, I sat down, in this "quiet phase" of my life, and wrote my life's story, which has been considered motivational by many. The truth be told, over the years, as I speak, teach and encourage others to pursue their dreams, I have shared my story with many people, and they find it both intriguing and inspiring. They are amazed to learn the struggles I have endured to become the person I am today. I am humbled by God's grace in my life. As a young girl and even as a young woman, so much happened to me to block my path. People weren't always friendly, and I had to kick some doors down, using the arsenal of education, optimism and the pleasant personality stored within me. Another thing that helped me was I never treated people as though they were less than me, regardless of the titles I carried.

How could this country girl not feel blessed and thankful when remembering from whence and how far I have come? It's unbelievable to me how people who have achieved a great deal in life soon forget how they got there and who helped them along the way. I believe in that famous line from Meditation XVII by the English poet John Donne, "No Man Is an Island entire of itself," that is, without a mentor or a person who offers words of encouragement or inspires self-confidence. Having this type of mind frame, took me much further in life, where I've been favored to be in the presence of some phenomenal people, such as our forty-second President, William Jefferson "Bill" Clinton, women's rights and civil rights activist and educator, the late Dr. Dorothy Height, and the award-winning actress and veteran of many acclaimed feature films and television series, Victoria Rowell, to name just a few. I will elaborate more on the influences that these renowned people have had on my life later in the book.

My story reflects the impact that desegregation and my school closing had on me during my formative years in Prince Edward County, Virginia, as well as on my later years. As a Southern country girl, I went through life without a roadmap, but trail blazed through it with optimism, high self-expectations and a belief in God to become an honor student and a proud parent of two successful daughters, as well as a foster parent to over one hundred foster boys over a twenty-year time period.

I have never been the type of person who merely talks a good talk or complains about what someone else should do about a problem or a situation; I put action behind my words. I hope this book is motivational and informative to the reader and gives insight into what times were like in the past; but, more importantly, shows the reader how anyone can turn their struggles and their setbacks into an inspiring plan of action for their life. Also, that their action plan can result in an exciting and rewarding career if they ditch the excuses and perform the hard work necessary to make their dreams a reality.

Love and blessings,
Aunt Hattie

Low Aim Is Sin

*"It must be borne in mind that
the tragedy of life doesn't lie in not reaching your goal.
The tragedy lies in having no goal to reach.
It isn't a calamity to die with dreams unfulfilled,
but it is a calamity not to dream.
It is not a disaster to be unable to capture your ideal,
but it is a disaster to have no ideal to capture.
It is not a disgrace not to reach the stars,
but it is a disgrace to have no stars to reach for.
Not failure, but low aim is sin."*

– BENJAMIN ELIJAH MAYS

~ PART ONE ~

Faith and Family

Jesus looked at them and said, "With man this is impossible, but with God all things are possible."
– MATTHEW 19:26 (NIV)

The beautiful picture my granddaughter, Reagan, drew of me and the optimism of my flight—being in God's hands at the end of His rainbow. I titled it *Above the Clouds*.

CHAPTER 1

The First Wave of the Baby Boomers:
Aiming to Make a Difference

*The more you praise and celebrate your life,
the more there is in life to celebrate.*

– OPRAH WINFREY

Yes! I am in the first wave of the Baby Boomers. The United States Census considers a baby boomer to be someone born during the demographic birth boom between 1946 and 1964. President Barack Obama, President Bill Clinton and his wife, Hillary Clinton, Oprah Winfrey, Bill Gates, Denzel Washington, Jimmy Buffett, Ellen DeGeneres, Branford Marsalis, and Mary Barra are all part of this special generation. We are the largest cohort of Americans born in U.S. history. My personal interpretation: We are that extraordinary generation that though we encountered trials and setbacks along the way, persisted, triumphed and brought about a change not only for our baby-boomer generation but also for future generations to come.

While I'm up above the clouds in an airplane en route to Florida from Baltimore, visiting my seven-year-old and ten-year-old granddaughters to attend Grandparents' Day at their elementary school, my heart is filled with unspeakable joy. God has truly blessed me and allowed me to be a blessing to others. Although it is a cloudy day, the sun above the clouds streams in through the airplane's window with its multicolored beams of light. I have this calming and serene feeling of magically floating above the clouds. My eyes are closed, experiencing a spiritual feeling of being carried by God to my next destination in life—whatever that may be and whatever He has in store for me.

My earthly problems are being controlled by my Heavenly Father, and He is telling me everything is going to be okay if I just keep the faith. I feel a sense of power knowing that God made this universe and is in control of the weather, the seasons, the leaves, the grass, the cherry blossoms, and every living creature. God is in control of each day, and He decides the timeline of these uncontrollable events and circumstances. *Since I believe and have faith in God,* I thought, *why then would I have more confidence in the pilot of this plane getting me to my destination than my God, who created the entire universe?* I settle back and feel that this is another sign that I had asked God to show me about my life's journey and the meaning of things that have happened in my life.

~

A couple hours later, I arrive at my daughter's house. She already knows my sad story, after many days on the phone with her. I needed a listening ear to get through this sad period in my life. After being open for just three years, Aunt Hattie's Place (AHP), a new third "eco-friendly" group home in Sandy Spring, Maryland, along with numerous other group homes in the state, is being reduced, sparked by a statewide initiative called Place Matters. The initiative was designed to keep children in families first and decrease the numbers of children in congregate care. Subsequently, this lack of state funding necessitated having to sell the boys group home and my personal home to pay off the construction loan.

My daughter puts her hand on my shoulder as she consoles and encourages me. I tell her like I've told others, I'm disappointed, but I'm also honored and feel blessed to have been able to help so many troubled teens from becoming another saddened statistic, especially black males. The reason I care so much for black males is that even long after the civil rights marches of the sixties and Martin Luther King, Jr.'s "I Have a Dream" speech, people of color continue to be disproportionately incarcerated, policed, and sentenced to death at significantly higher rates than their white counterparts. According to the Bureau of Justice Statistics, one in three black men can expect to go to prison in their lifetime. Very troubling and dismal statistics, indeed, and they don't appear to be getting any better.

Anxious to make a difference in the community and the world, I founded my first group home for foster boys, Aunt Hattie's Place (AHP), in 1997. The boys, who were abused, neglected and/or abandoned, were overjoyed to stay at Aunt Hattie's Place. While at AHP, they were able to attend public or private schools, eat three home-cooked meals a day and stay in a clean, clutter-free environment. AHP's staff implemented rules and offered guidance and structure that were very different from the surroundings the boys had left.

Although the recently built Aunt Hattie's Place group home for boys in Sandy Spring is closed, I remain grateful to have another residential group home for foster boys in Baltimore City. Having the opportunity to mentor young people, has allowed me to move forward on my never-ending journey of making a difference and helping people just like others helped me.

Meanwhile, my granddaughter, Reagan (our budding artist in the family), is listening quietly to the entire conversation and drawing a picture as she frequently does. After finishing, she presents me with the picture that she drew. It captured everything I had said to her mom, along with her special embellishments.

My eyes become glassy with tears. The drawing has me looking out of the airplane at the clouds below with a large rainbow encircling the plane. At each end of the rainbow, she has penned the word "God." She explains that God is taking care of me, because she constantly prays for me and my foster boys every night. I am too touched and too full to respond. I give her the biggest hug and compliment her on capturing the essence of our entire conversation so well and exactly the way grandma feels.

I take this event as another sign from God that He oversees His plan for me, and for me to just be still and patient. Another takeaway is that out of the mouths of babes, God speaks through His children. Therefore, it behooves His people to listen and to understand what He is trying to reveal to us.

After our conversation, I reflect on my life and the rich tapestry of it that has defined the person I am today, a past filled with triumphs as well as challenges. At one point in my life, I felt in order to overcome the feeling of loneliness and betrayal, I used my fond memories of early childhood as medicine to cope with the pain. Many people allow roadblocks to defeat them causing them to give up, but I decided a long time ago to learn from the challenges placed before me. These challenges have made me stronger and more resilient.

Tenacity and courage have always run deeply through my veins; and, believe me, I have had my share of hardships. When people seemingly had low expectations of me, I would turn those low expectations and negative attitudes around to be a reverse motivator for me. I would contemplate an "I'll show you" attitude.

Then, I would have faith in God, faith in myself and would work hard and make it happen. I've learned through the years that everything happens for a reason. My pastor, Reverend Haywood A. Robinson, III of The People's Community Baptist Church in Maryland, has frequently reinforced this perspective lesson to me by remarking, "The Lord closes one door and opens another one." When I was younger, I heard my father say numerous times, "What doesn't kill you, makes you stronger."

~

It was nearly twenty years ago, during which time I was assistant superintendent of Baltimore Schools when the mission of Aunt Hattie's Place was originated. During that time, my personal home was licensed as a foster home and I became a foster mom. To me, it seems like only yesterday that I was driving down Park Heights Avenue in my school district. I was out visiting different schools, when I soon noticed three youths, who looked to be in their early teens, standing on the street corner. I glanced at my watch and quickly realized that schools were still in session. Being not only the assistant superintendent, but also a concerned mother, I drove up to the young black teens and stopped the car. I rolled down the window and said very authoritatively, "Excuse me, young men. Why are you out of school?"

All three boys looked at one another, and then looked at me as if to say, "Who are you?" I continued and said, "I am the assistant superintendent of the Baltimore City Schools System. This is my school district, and you're standing on my streets in the middle of the day. Therefore, I am going to ask you one more time, why aren't you in school? And, which school should you be attending anyway?"

The bigger boy, who seemed older than the other two, said, "My name is Jonathan, and these are my friends Charles and Jerome. They have nowhere to go. They are out of school until their social workers can find them a place to stay." He said, in effect, that they didn't know which school to attend because they didn't have an actual home address.

After hearing that and the fact that one of the boys had been out of school for weeks, my mouth widened, and my eyes grew large with astonishment. Being a concerned parent and not wanting to see my children on the street homeless, let alone someone else's child, I instinctively told all three boys to get inside my car.

At first, they were hesitant, which I could understand. I gave them credit for being cautious with me being a stranger, but after sensing my concern and my authoritative demand to get in the car, they complied. It also didn't hurt that they were offered a meal from McDonald's down the street when they said they were hungry. Two climbed in the backseat, and the older one slid in the front. I rarely go to McDonald's for myself. I prefer a home-cooked meal instead of fast food, but I had no time to waste and had to make a quick decision on what to do about the boys.

Ten minutes later, I phoned my secretary and explained to her the situation. I instructed her not only to cancel my appointments for the rest of the day, but also to call social services immediately. I wanted to get to the bottom of this situation. How could children be out of school day after day, for weeks even, and no one reports their absence, has concern that they are missing, nor is anyone looking for them?

During the ride to McDonald's, I respectively learned their ages—eleven, twelve, and thirteen. The older one acted as if he were the big brother, carrying all the responsibilities that came with the job. He seemed to get more comfortable with me and commented that I had a nice car. I asked him if he were homeless, too. He shook his head, as he reclined the seat and sat back relaxed as if we'd known each other for years and were just traveling out of town. Then, he told me that he stayed with his grandmother, and he secretly lets his friends (he pointed his head toward the backseat) stay downstairs in his grandmother's basement, since they had nowhere else to go. I told him that was kind of him, but that he still needed to be in school. He quickly informed me that he goes to school whenever he feels like it, and that today was a day he didn't feel like going.

After the leader of the pack shared his reason for not going to school, I began experiencing all kinds of emotions ranging from sadness to anger. I hated to see youth in dire situations and even worse, them not caring about their education. More importantly, as a former teacher, I was also concerned that they felt nothing interesting or fun was happening in school, which is why they went when they felt like it. I felt confident these young black boys could have bright futures if they had the appropriate mentors in their lives to change their ways of thinking. Without these, they could become part of the criminal justice system, or even worse, dead.

~

Later, after leaving the McDonald's drive-thru, while the boys were munching on cheeseburgers and fries, they were talking among themselves about football and basketball. I heard one of them say, "When I grow up, I'm going to play for the Baltimore Ravens." Then, I heard the leader of the pack respond jokingly, "In your dreams. My grandmother stands a better chance of getting on the Raven's team than you." The youngest one, who also happened to be the quietest one, laughed aloud.

I looked in the rearview mirror at the two of them and said, "You can be anything you want to be as long as you believe in yourself and do the work to get there." They didn't respond to my words of encouragement but appeared to be pondering the message—as if no one had ever believed in them or given them hope for their future.

Jonathan took a bite out of his burger and then turned his head and gazed out of the passenger's side window, seemingly in deep thought. I touched him on the shoulder as I felt what he was thinking. He turned around quickly and looked at me with woeful eyes. I said, "And you can, too." He nodded skeptically, and then turned back to the passenger's window.

I thought for a moment, was my meeting these boys a chance

meeting or divine intervention? Subsequent to meeting these boys on the street, I called a special meeting with all my principals in my northwest school district and required them to email me daily the names of all students who were absent from school that day. Going one step further, I also wanted the names of the teachers who had called out absent. Several teachers would be out notoriously on Mondays and Fridays, and this was not acceptable in my school district.

I was mindful of the fact that many students came from dysfunctional families and needed a constant nurturing environment during the weekdays at school. Many students witness violence in their neighborhood and at home, then when returning to school and not seeing their regular teacher, but a substitute teacher, instead, add to their feeling of instability and their disenchantment with school. The students could develop a negative attitude that their very own teachers weren't that enthused themselves about coming to school.

I parked the car in my designated parking space and turned to the boys and said, "Let's go inside." All of us got out the car, and they followed me inside my office. I told them to wait for me in there, pointing to the lovely small cozy room beside my office that was painted pink on purpose. During my years of teaching special education students, I learned from experience that colors have various effects on people. The "pink room" is one of my initiatives that I've used with students who have severe learning and behavioral problems. Since I've done this for quite a while, I feel it's my calling. Many of these techniques will be shared in another part of this book.

The boys acted like little gentlemen. They sat beside the knee-high coffee table where I had *National Geographic* magazines and a small glass container filled with mints. The candy jar had a sign taped to the front of it that read, "You're Worth a Mint." In the background, there was soft music playing. The room had lovely white sheer lace curtains with a pink valance that hung down on each side of the wide window in a swag shape. There was a white throw rug under the coffee table that matched the curtains and throw pillows on the beige sofa. The color pink and the pleasant surroundings in that room had a calming effect on children who were angry, as well as irate parents.

My pink room was such a success that many of my principals created their own "pink room" in their schools. Since I had challenged my principals with an innovative initiative not to suspend any students for minor behavioral incidents, but implement alternative approaches within their school building first, many principals decided that a "pink room" was worth a try. Subsequently, if the principals could not change the student's inappropriate behavior over a reasonable period of time, they were then to refer the student to my office.

~

After I saw that the boys were settled, I quickly moved into my office and placed my purse on my desk. My secretary walked in and handed me a sticky note. Then the news that I wasn't expecting to hear, spoke forth from her lips: "Social Services said those boys are runaways."

I looked at her with stunned eyes. "Are they looking for a home for them? What does that mean?"

She shrugged her shoulders and portrayed an incredulous look on her face. I narrowed my eyes at her, thinking, I can't just return these boys to the street corner and let them wander like stray dogs. They weren't stray dogs they were human beings, who needed guidance, nurturing and, most of all, love. My heart just wouldn't allow it. I shook my head thinking of the boys' welfare. My mind was in rambling mode. Before the board meeting, I called the number that my secretary gave me and asked them about the timeline for finding a home for these boys.

Because these boys had a record of being perpetual runaways, called AWOLs (Absence Without Leave), I was given the impression that Social Services wasn't in a hurry to place the boys in a home. The boys didn't seem like they were in a hurry to be placed in one either.

Hours later, I had not heard back from Social Services and it was almost time for my board meeting. I ended up bringing Charles and Jerome, the two youngest boys, with me to my board meeting. Jonathan, the oldest one, went back home to his grandmother. At the board meeting, I gave each one an assignment so that they wouldn't get bored. I had purchased a pair of disposable cameras from the drug store before we arrived. I instructed them to take photos and notes on what each speaker was saying and to write a brief description of what they heard. After the meeting, they showed me what they had written. I realized that these young men weren't dumb at all. They had followed the instructions that I had given them and did an outstanding job. I knew then that if these two young teens had some reinforcement or intervention, they could achieve anything they wanted to be.

Later that evening, we drove to my home in the county. I owned a four-bedroom house, and I thought that I would provide a place for the m to lay their heads for that one night. At the time, both of my daughters were away at college, and I had three empty bedrooms.

Most people today wouldn't think of bringing children they knew nothing about to their home. It's uncommon. However, I grew up in a black community during a time where relatives or even non-relatives would take in a child or another person who needed a reprieve for a few days, a few weeks, months and even years. Known as community mothers and extended families, these people looked out for and helped raised other people's children.

They went faithfully by the Bible verse Philippians 2:4 "Not looking to your own interests but each of you to the interests of others." Anyone in the community could speak to and reprimand a child and were welcomed if they informed the parents of the child acting inappropriately. Many non-blood relationships were respectfully referred to as "Aunts" and "Uncles." The same type of love and nurturing that was in our close-knit community was the catalyst behind starting Aunt Hattie's Place where all the staff, board members, volunteers, and supporters are called "Aunt" or "Uncle."

That night, I showed both boys their sleeping quarters. They were so happy to be there, apparent by the smiles on their faces. Their smiles struck a chord with me. We instantly had a connection. I trusted them and, most importantly, they trusted me.

I washed their clothes and cooked them a delicious home-cooked meal. Before bed, we sat around the kitchen table and talked. I told them that they could be anything they wanted to be, that they were smart boys and not to let anyone tell them otherwise, regardless of their circumstances now. I even showed them all the sets of books I had by Grolier: *The World's Great Classics, The Health & Medical Books, The Books of Popular Science,* and *The Geography & Social Studies Books* that my daughters read when they were in middle and high school. They were amazed at the number of books my daughters had to read. One of the boys said, "They really read all these books?" I nodded and replied, "They sure did."

I sat on the edge of the bed and reiterated what I had told them earlier, about being anything they wanted to be if they first believed it and were willing to work hard and get a good education. In doing so, I thought back to my elementary school teacher, Mrs. Brown, a charming black woman who had taken me home after school to spend the night. I remember that I was no more than 10 years old. That experience forever changed my life. She was my favorite teacher and probably the biggest influence in my desire to become a teacher.

In my teacher's warm, comfortable house, I slept by myself in a bed for the first time, not nestled with three other siblings as I was accustomed to at home. Her bed had two sheets with a comforter, something that was new to me at the time, as I was used to a bed having only one sheet that was a makeshift sheet that Mama had sewn together from feed, called "shiftstuff" bags. Also, at home, I had on my bed a couple of quilts that were handmade by Aunt Mildred and Aunt Mary, relatives of Mama's late husband.

Mrs. Brown's guest room bed literally felt like heaven and was so very soft and comfy that I felt like the covers were hugging me, as if I were floating on clouds. I'll never forget. This same floating-on-the-clouds happy feeling is the feeling I felt earlier. It's so amazing how memories of incidents and experiences in the past can be recalled by sights, smells, and sounds in the present. That's why it is crucial to concentrate on how you make children "feel" as they are growing up.

They need to feel loved, feel connected to a person, and feel self-worth, regardless of how rich or poor they are. If they feel loved and special, that's all that they will remember years later: the feeling, not the food that they ate at the time or what they were wearing or any of those insignificant facts. Many times, they will remember the pleasant music, certain songs and scents (just like I remember Mrs. Brown's perfume that brings back a happy feeling) that will forever be a part of their well-being or conversely, be part of their depressed or dysfunctional well-being.

After dinner, Mrs. Brown sat on the side of the bed, for no more than ten minutes. Those ten minutes are permanently ingrained in my memory and in my spirit. She gently took my hand while telling me what she saw in me. At ten years old, my mouth widened at her powerful words. I had no idea what I was or who I was. I was astonished like, wow, she sees those attributes in me? In a soft loving voice, she told me that one day, I'd make a great teacher, that I was smart, and that I could be anything that I wanted to be. Mrs. Brown provided me with positive motivation that prepared me for further education. I gained tremendous confidence from my relationship with her, who I consider one of my "Mentor Mothers" that helped fuel all my subsequent successes.

By the power and grace of God, I was able to learn from and

overcome many obstacles to accomplish some great feats and firsts in my lifetime. I was the first in my immediate family to graduate from high school and the first to graduate from college. I was the first African-American Parent Teacher Association (PTA) President of the elementary school my older daughter attended. I was the first parent to be PTA President for several years from the time my daughters were in middle school and through high school.

~

Additionally, I had the honor and privilege of being the first female vice president (VP) of Coppin State University for eight years, and I helped raise over $8 million for the university, when the goal was only $3 million, thanks to a hand-picked staff.

Prior to being the VP of Coppin, I was the assistant superintendent of Baltimore City Schools in Baltimore, Maryland, where the vision of Aunt Hattie's Place originated. In addition to those career achievements, I've been a local state administrator, college professor, TV hostess, a civic activist, a special education teacher, and a teacher in the United States and abroad.

~

The next day, I called Social Services again and told them to call me if they found the boys a home. Each day, I or my secretary would call Social Services to see if there was a home for the boys, and would let them know that I still had them staying with me. I would bring them each morning with me to my area office. After several days and no home yet, I called the principal of the middle school next door to my annex office and asked him to select one of his best teachers to teach the boys temporarily until I could find them a home.

The principal was happy to oblige because he felt the same way as I did about wasted brainpower of young boys who were lost and seemingly felt hopeless, and that no one cared about whether they were in school or not.

I also met with the area police department and businesses and asked them to notify me, if they saw any kids walking around during the day. I was going to crackdown on attendance. No child should be on the street corner standing around when their future depended on them being in school and learning.

During their stay, I eventually received a call from Social Services, several weeks later, asking me if I still had foster kids staying at my home and telling me that I couldn't just take foster kids home and keep them. I was told that I needed to be trained to be a foster parent and that my house had to be inspected and licensed as a foster home. I was flabbergasted. I thought, Mrs. Brown just took me home to spend the night and changed my life forever. Why can't I just pay it forward and return the good deed to these young teens, as she and others had done for me? Why did I need a license to keep homeless kids?

"Let me see if I understand what you are saying," I said, mystified. I had no knowledge at that time of the workings and requirements to be a foster parent. I just wanted to give the boys a home for a few nights. I didn't want, nor did I plan to become a foster parent. I said, "You mean to tell me that this very same house where I have raised two daughters, who are now in college, must now be inspected and licensed to keep foster boys that I picked up off the streets, boys whom no one was looking for?" Further, I indicated that I had a doctorate and taught school for years and that I felt insulted to be mandated to keep these homeless youth. I could not see the logic in this process requirement when the need was imminent.

Needless to say, I took the twelve-hour training course requirement and even assisted the instructor to do much of the teaching—as this was my area of expertise. Next, my home had to be certified. Inspectors came to check the temperature in the refrigerator and the tap water and measure the rooms, making sure the house was suitable for foster children. In no time, my personal haven became certified and licensed as a therapeutic foster home.

At one of my board meetings, one of my colleagues asked me if the boys were still staying with me. I told him yes. If I planned to keep them for an extended period of time, the colleague recommended that it would be wise to open a group home for foster boys because I could obtain more resources and personnel to assist with their needs.

It became necessary to hire a housekeeper to cook, clean and care for the boys due to my grueling schedule. I didn't anticipate keeping them for this long. I wanted them to have some semblance of a normal day after school rather than going with me to board meetings, PTA meetings at my schools and other events; therefore, this person temporarily served that purpose. However, coming home late one night after an exhausting day and even more tiresome board meeting, the boys were waiting up for me, sitting on the steps to the family room. "Hi, guys," I greeted them. "Why are you still up?" I asked them. "Can we talk to you?" one of them asked. Even though I was tired, the look on their faces made me concerned about what was going on, and I replied, "Sure, what is it?"

One quietly and emotionally, asked me with all sincerity, "Do you know why my mother put me in foster care and kept my sister? Do you think she loves her better than me?" Before, I could think of what to say to him, the other young man asked me, "Do you think when my daddy gets out of jail, he will come looking for me? Will he want me back?" he asked with such a lonesome sadness that chills went through me and tears welled up in my eyes.

I had no answers for them. I was bone tired, and I knew then these kids needed more than a meal and a place to sleep. They needed some psychological counseling and therapy. The only thing I could think to do at that moment was to say, "Can I have a hug? I need a hug."

They readily complied. I felt that that was what they needed and didn't know how to express the loneliness, the longing and the craving for love and belonging somewhere and to somebody.

I could indeed relate to their feeling of abandonment and being uprooted and not knowing the reason. I felt like this when I was uprooted in 1959 when the schools closed for five years in Prince Edward County due to desegregation. These insurmountable emotional and psychological issues, with which they were wrestling, were beyond my training and expertise—not to mention the time allotment needed to address their past experience of abandonment and hurt. I knew then that if I planned to keep these young men and raise them to be successful and productive citizens—which I knew they had the potential to be—that I needed more help, resources, and staff. To that end, I took the board member's advice and pursued opening a group home to provide these wraparound services to these deserving young men.

~

Reflecting back, my psychological mindset was that I would not live much past the age of 27, which was my biological mother's age when she died. This instinct propelled me yet again to make bold moves early in life and gave me the impetus and the foresight to make a difference in life. My instinct helped me choose mentor mothers, like Mrs. Brown, and others who demonstrated traits that I would imagine in my own mother whom I had never witnessed because she died when I was only three years old. Sometimes these persons, whom I had chosen, knew they were my mentor mothers and fathers, and many times, they did not know I had chosen them as a role model. I tried to emulate their positive character, behavior, speech, mannerisms, aspirations and other behaviors that I imagined my mother would have possessed and that I wished to have myself.

I encourage everyone, especially disadvantaged children, to find someone they admire who has a positive and inspirational outlook on life and is accomplished and emulate them. I have found that most times successful people consider it an honor, a sheer act of flattery when someone wants to be like them. More people should try asking for mentorship throughout their life, and they will soon discover more help is available than they could have imagined.

*If you can't fly, then run,
If you can't run, then walk, If you can't walk, then crawl,
But whatever you do, you have to keep moving forward.*

– DR. MARTIN LUTHER KING, JR.

CHAPTER 2

Where It All Began

*And we know that for those who love God
all things work together for good, for those who
are called according to his purpose.*

– ROMANS 8:28 (NIV)

The story of my life began in the wee hours of the morning in 1946 in Norfolk, Virginia. I am the daughter of Samuel Neal, Jr., a former Navy man, and Janie Lucille Goganious Neal, a homemaker. My brother and sisters were born between 1945 and 1948. My mother died when I was too young to remember her. To this day, my mother's death is still a mystery. Her sister, Hattie, after whom I was named, thinks she died from complications of childbirth or heart problems. Aunt Hattie is the matriarch of the family. I will take what she says as truth. Although I had no recall of my mother's face, to hear it from relatives, I resemble her.

My Aunt Hattie told me that my father was smitten with my mother from the moment he first laid eyes on her. I am told by several older relatives that my mother was a very beautiful, unassuming woman with a striking face. With her small waistline, proportionate hips, breasts and her tall shapely legs, she had a distinct presence when she entered any room. Her presence caused both men and women to look up and wonder, "Whooo is that?" I understand that she had this aura and a certain mystique about her that was all her own, punctuated by this certain walk, a smooth graceful sway, hitting the floor balanced and sultry—poetry in motion, as some have said. The walk revealed I am confident and comfortable in my own skin and I am in this moment, right here, right now; I own this space at this time.

~

Trying to deduce her persona as she has been described to me by other relatives, I concluded that she was not antisocial nor was she considered social, but she had what was akin to an asocial personality. This characteristic portrayed my mother as being comfortable both alone and comfortable with others. As my Aunt Hattie put it frankly, "That is, those with whom she chose to let into her inner circle of conversation and interaction." My mother didn't feel the need to be the center of attention. Nor was she verbose or aggressive, so I was told. She was rather reserved, but not shy; was confident, but not snooty; was knowledgeable on many subjects, but not gregarious or flamboyant, but could hold a conversation with anyone on any level when she was approached.

Aunt Hattie told me that my mother could be mistaken for being egocentric; however, she was far from it. In fact, she had a very warm and caring heart and felt empathy for the underdog and the downtrodden. Aunt Hattie said that my mother once cooked a complete meal for a person considered to be a "tramp" that would go from house to house in the community and beg for food and clothes. She set the table for him like he was the king of England. Aunt Hattie asked her, "Why are you doing that for a tramp?" My mother responded, "Because he could be an angel of God. You never know who you're entertaining."

I feel my birth mother is constantly with me—my guardian angel, protecting me from harm.

~

My father, Samuel Neal, Jr., my hero, was part Indian and mixed with another ethnic background besides black, possibly Greek or German, so I was told. My father had a strong, distinctive accent. It wasn't the ordinary Southern accent. His accent made him stand out among the rest. He was a broad-shouldered, ambitious man whose personal courage in the face of impossible odds inspired me to want to do well in life. Despite him only having a fifth-grade formal education and teaching himself what I feel is the equivalent to a college curriculum, he did not allow his lack of education to deter him from making money. The man, who owned a lumber business in a small town where mostly whites owned businesses, was passionate about providing well for his family. He was also passionate about his children receiving adequate education. Raised on a farm, his father passed his skills of farming to him. Back then, my father had fields of corn, strings beans, tomato, cucumber, squash, and watermelon. My family never missed a meal. A mild-mannered man and church trustee, my father, loved mostly everyone with whom he came into contact and got along well with everyone in our small Southern community. And, it was no different in our household.

He would take turns carrying my sisters and me on his wide shoulders around the yard. We'd fight over who would get to climb on Daddy's back first. In the evening, we would gather in the living room after supper. My father would sit on a wooden stool, and we'd all rush to sit at his feet. He'd roll up his sleeves and tell us stories, using animals, about his workday. Seeing him roll up his sleeves, as he began to tell us his stories, let us know that he was going to become animated and dramatize various parts of the story, at times rising from the stool and flapping his arms in the air to make a point. Filled with excitement and visual imaginaries of his descriptions, my siblings and I would listen intently to these short stories he'd make up for us to enjoy. For example, he would tell us that while in the woods cutting down trees, a bear would approach him and say, "You can't cut down that tree. That's my favorite tree." Then, the "momma bear" would climb down and offer him dinner. He said that he would decline momma bear's offer and told her that he had supper at his house waiting on him. He had us kids thinking that these animals really talked.

I used to love it when my father told us stories. As a little girl, it was always my favorite time with my father because he worked many hours at his lumber business and the small store he owned in town a few miles from our house. He was a great storyteller. Not only would he make up his own fictional stories, but also, he would read us Uncle Remus stories about Brer Rabbit out of a big storybook he'd have in the palms of his big callus-riddled hands. My favorite story was the story of Tar-Baby, the tale where Brer Fox constructs a doll out of a lump of tar and puts clothes on it. It isn't long until Brer Rabbit encounters the doll, and because the doll doesn't talk back, Brer Rabbit becomes frustrated, punches it and gets stuck. Then here comes Brer Fox contemplating on how to dispose of Brer Rabbit.

My father should have been a comedian because every time he told that story, along with other tales, he'd crack up himself. His laughter was infectious. He'd have us, kids, laughing and asking him to finish the story. Laugh tears would stream down his face and ours, too. When I first heard him tell the Tar-Baby story, I was scared for Brer Rabbit, but after my father had informed me that rabbits are at home in thickets and that Brer Rabbit really wanted Brer Fox to put him in there—I thought, how smart of Brer Rabbit. I remember my father would have me dying laughing when he would portray Brer Rabbit. He'd say, "Please, Brer Fox don't throw me in dat dar briar patch."

To this day, my father's bedtime stories still amuse me. Even though my father has passed, his stories are forever embedded in my heart and memory. I shared his stories with my daughters when they were growing up and now with my granddaughters, foster boys, and anyone who loves to listen to good storytelling. It's a pity that the art of storytelling is lost today and is not as engaging as it used to be because of the many distractions and electronic preoccupation and interferences.

~

In my father's late twenties, after my mother died, and I was just three, he met and later married a very young woman, Hilda "Teenie" Lee. She was a pretty lady who loved my siblings and me dearly. Out of all my siblings and her own children, I felt as if I were her favorite. "Mama," as I called her, never released from her lips that I was her favorite, but I always perceived it through her warm smile and the nice things she would do for me. She had an endearing way of standing beside me and putting her hand on my shoulder. If I were greasing the bread pan or setting our kitchen table, she would touch my shoulder, and her very soft touch made me feel so loved, so nurtured. And she was a hugger, too.

I recall coming home from school or church when all my siblings and I would run to her, and she'd grab all of us up in her arms and give us the warmest hug. I laugh to myself every time I think of the way she hugged us. She was doing the "group hug" back then, even before society has come to realize the power and therapy of a hug. I read on the Internet that there are people who earn a living from hugging and snuggling others in a non-sexual way. They are known as professional cuddlers, making anywhere from $60 an hour to $300 a night to spoon, hug or snuggle with a client. I find that intriguing because many public schools have a "no hugging" policy. I feel that schools shouldn't implement this policy. We all need human contact. Students, especially students with behavior problems, need a good hug from a teacher. The health benefits of touch are known to relieve stress, to lower blood pressure and to build healthy relationships. Besides, children know the difference between healthy affection and unwanted sexual behavior, for the most part.

~

Mama's story was much the same as my father's. She was born in rural Virginia and had no extensive formal education beyond elementary school. She was a very smart and loving woman. My fondest memories were coming home after school. Mama would have it smelling so good inside our home. There was always something cooking that would flatter your nose and taste buds. She'd say, "Change from out of your school clothes and come back down, and dinner will be ready."

Mama was a great cook. I remembered she would cook her own special recipes of classic Southern dishes, such as mouth-watering stew and chicken and dumplings, to corn fritters, fried apple turnovers, and gingerbread. Her homemade gingerbread was to die for. She'd make it from scratch with just the right amount of flour, eggs, sugar, ginger, grandma molasses, and other spices like nutmeg and cinnamon. Her gingerbread was a cross between a brownie, a gingersnap and a piece of chocolate cake. The memories and the time spent with Mama in the kitchen as she cooked helped shape my life. Because of her, I not only became a great cook of her special recipes, but I also knew that one day I wanted to be a nurturing mother and homemaker, just like she was.

A naturally beautiful black woman, with high cheekbones and long coal-black hair that was slightly curly at the ends, Mama wore her hair in a large bun. Many times, she'd say, "Sistah, go get the comb and scratch my head." I'd stop whatever I was doing, because I loved being close to her. I'd smile and go grab the comb. I felt so special, back then. My eight-year-old body would pull up a kitchen chair to her. I would sit in it with her sitting on our wooden floor, and I would scratch her scalp. Scratching her scalp, I felt relieved her of some of the tension she was feeling from taking care of a husband and house filled with children. Or, maybe scratching her head relieved her from a long day of cooking and cleaning from early morning to evening. I remember Mama smiling with her eyes closed, head draped to the side and her falling asleep like a baby.

I loved Mother's Day. My siblings and I made Mama homemade cards and clay figurines from school. We would pick apples, peaches and cherries from the trees, alongside the roads, and give them to her and my father's cousins, Aunt Mamie and Aunt Pauline. (Out of respect, we were raised to call elders "Aunt" even when they were just cousins or close friends of the family). Both aunts lived a few miles away. We had to travel through the fields to get to their house. Aunt Mamie and Aunt Pauline would bake apple, peach, and cherry pies from the fruits we had given them. The pies would smell so good. Mama was so proud of us. After admiring her gifts, she'd smile and kiss and thank us for the wonderful gifts.

The times that I spend with my daughters and granddaughters during Mother's Day remind me of those days with Mama. My daughter, Cheryl, and my oldest foster son, Wayne, usually take me to brunch for Mother's Day and any other "just because" occasion. We sit, eat and just talk and laugh for hours. My older daughter, Charrell, who resides in another state, and her family never miss sending flowers and lovely touching cards in the mail. I enjoy those times tremendously.

~

I am no longer the eight-year-old child I was then. I'm a grown woman, and I find myself doing many things that my Mama used to do. Parents don't realize either directly or indirectly how kids pick up their habits/rituals, good, bad or indifferent. For example, Mama used to place rice in her saltshaker. I never knew why then. I learned later in high school chemistry class that rice was a hygroscopic material, meaning it absorbs water, moisture, and odor. I'm thinking these country people from way back when knew some things. I find myself doing that to this day. Mama would also place an open box of baking soda in the refrigerator. I do that, too, and discovered later that baking soda eliminates and absorbs odors and keeps food fresh. She'd put a pinch of salt in her coffee and added plenty of cream and sugar.

That's the way I like my coffee today. She would also put a pinch of salt on her cantaloupe, her tomatoes, watermelon and cucumber—I do the same to this day, except I use sea salt rather than iodized salt, almond milk rather than regular milk, Truvia rather than white sugar. Mama and Daddy would turn over in their graves after hearing about these "sugar and milk substitutes," as they were real milk and real sugar connoisseurs.

CHAPTER 3

Massive Resistance in a Small Town:
School Closings

"Efforts and courage are not enough without purpose and direction."

– JFK

I learned in my childhood years that no one is immune from heartache. There were times in my life where I had to remake and reshape my life, a life punctuated periodically by pain and heartache. I had to accept certain things that I could not change, one being segregation. I grew up during a time where being black was like having the black plague. As a child and all through my teenage years, I could not wrap my head around what was the fear in not wanting another human being to go to school, sit at a lunch counter, ride the bus, drink from the same water fountain, and use the same public restroom with white people. Why? Really, what was the fear? I could not comprehend the meaning of racism and the premise thereof.

I recalled at Levi Elementary School, every morning, my class would religiously recite the Pledge of Allegiance ". . . one Nation under God, with liberty and justice for all." I believed in these words and the ideas back then. As a student, I was taught American History, which covered the civil war, the Emancipation Proclamation that freed the slaves, and Christian-based dogma. It was these very ideas that made America the country that other nations strived to emulate, and other diverse people wanted to come to, even illegally, and become American citizens.

The summer of 1959, when I was thirteen years old, was a summer that forever changed me and my view of the world. It was an evening when everyone was settled in the house. I knew something was terribly wrong seeing the image on my father's face. My father, the solid man who served his country during World War II, traveling turbulent seas onboard a navy ship, had a nervous, almost petrified look on his face that evening. He told us the schools would be closing indefinitely and that he was sending us to Norfolk, Virginia, so we could continue to go to school. I remember it like it was yesterday. My body instantly became limp. I was too shocked to cry. Then my mind went into rambling mode. Norfolk, I thought. Where was Norfolk and who was in Norfolk? I didn't have to ask out loud. Apparently, my father saw the question marks written on my face, along with my siblings' faces. He said in a low, barely audible voice while looking at my brother, Samuel, and sister, Terrie, "Ya'll be staying with your real mother's sisters."

Hearing the news that I would be separated from most of my family wasn't confusing and troubling enough. Hearing the words, ya'll be staying with your real mother's sisters, felt like a jackhammer was being slammed into my stomach. I looked at Mama. Her eyes were lowered. Then, I looked at my father and said, "We'll be staying with Mama's sisters?"

"No," my father replied.

"Isn't Mama my mother?" I asked.

He said, "No. Your real mother died when you were three." He pointed at the woman I had been calling Mama. "This is your stepmother," he added.

I wanted to cry, but, again, I was too stunned to cry. I leaned over, touched my sister, and asked," Did you know that?" Terrie shook her head, looking as stunned as I did. I looked at my other brothers and sisters whom I had thought were my blood brothers and sisters, but soon learned they were not. I heard my father in the background explaining how he had met my stepmother and how she had six children before she married him. She had three Baileys: Claudzell, the oldest; Audrey "Tootie Boo"; next to the oldest, and Jerome "Bonky"; the youngest. Then she had three Lees: Larry, the oldest; Cledith "Clet" the middle child, and Sterling the youngest, all were my stepsiblings. I recall when Cledith left Meherrin. He went to Baltimore, Maryland and took a job as a janitor for a hamburger place. He later became cashier, then manager and finally owner of a Kentucky Fried Chicken restaurant. He eventually owned thirteen Kentucky Fried Chicken restaurants, as well as a Pep Boys and a few Taco Bell Franchises. Many of my stepbrothers worked for him, prior to his death.

All that evening, I replayed the things my father had told us, children—and then the tears began to flow. I lay on the bed and cried until I had no more tears left to shed. My eyes were red like the sun, my body was weak, and my heart was broken.

Looking back, the sole purpose of sending my siblings and me from our tight-village community—where everyone knew everyone and called each other Aunt, Uncle or Cousin—was to complete our education and pursue our career paths—and not sit idle for the next five years that the schools were closed in Prince Edward County. Though my father only went to the fifth grade himself, he valued education tremendously and did all he could to support the community and the National Association for the Advancement of Colored People (NAACP) during this desegregation process. He wanted his children to continue their education without an interruption—at all cost.

The thing that both confused and appalled me about the school closings was the hypocrisy of elected and appointed leaders, banding together to pass legislation that effectively closed down an entire school system rather than comply with the Justice Department by integrating the white students with us black students.

At the time, I didn't know the color of one's skin mattered, until I was faced with the traumatic experience of being sent away from my nurturing home environment at an early age for education's sake. Then there was my father, now, retired from service after proudly putting his life on the line for his country against the "enemy of war" only to come home to these supposedly "United" States and encounter the "enemy" here that wouldn't allow his children to go to school with the same people he risked his life and fought to protect their rights.

To provide you with a little U.S. history, as a perspective on what was happening in the country during my childhood: On May 17, 1954, when I was just eight years old, the United States Supreme Court, in a unanimous decision, declared state laws establishing separate public schools for black and white students was unconstitutional. The ruling meant that I would be taught in a classroom with not just black students, like myself, but also with white students. Desegregating public schools started with fearless people like Barbara Johns, niece of civil rights pioneer Reverend Vernon Johns, who was pastor of Montgomery's Dexter Avenue Baptist Church at the time. He was a civil rights advocate. Barbara Johns, a medium-height, ambitious girl, was just sixteen years old when she organized and led a two-week strike. Many students refused to attend classes.

As I mentioned in my Introduction, the reason for the two-week strike was that R. R. Moton High School, a high school, built in 1939 in Prince Edward County, Virginia, for African-American children, was heavily overcrowded by the 1950s. The conditions of the black schools were much worse than the white schools. The county tried to appease black students by building long buildings that looked like chicken coops to house the overflow. Barbara Johns and other students had had enough. They wrote the NAACP to help in their struggle for better conditions. The NAACP agreed to take the Prince Edward case only if the students and their parents would sue to desegregate the schools. The students and parents didn't mind suing to desegregate the schools if that's what it took to get better school facilities and better school conditions.

It wasn't long until, NAACP lawyers, including Oliver W. Hill, a civil rights attorney whose work against racial discrimination helped put an end to the doctrine "separate, but equal," came to Prince Edward County, Virginia on one sunny afternoon. The case, *Davis v. County School Board of Prince Edward County,* would turn out to bear some of the most significant attributes in the history of civil rights. The case advanced to the Supreme Court, along with four other cases from Delaware, South Carolina, and Washington, D.C. and the famous, *Brown v. Board of Education* case from Kansas that challenged segregation in public schools. All the cases combined became known as *Brown v. Board of Education.* The Supreme Court declared that segregation in public schools was unconstitutional. It was a landmark victory, but the state of Virginia was determined to make desegregating schools more difficult than it needed to be by imposing a policy of "massive resistance" that would effectively delay school desegregation until the 1960s.

When Prince Edward County Board of Supervisors voted not to fund the schools, the schools immediately closed. Teachers lost their jobs and families, like mine, were separated for education's sake.

Then there were those families whose children simply did not go to school, because the parents either couldn't afford to send them off, or the parents had nowhere for their children to go. Even though, my siblings and I were considered the fortunate ones, as we had somewhere to go to receive an education, our picture-postcard family was separated. I would no longer see my father or the woman

I had known as my mother, the love of my life. Also, I was being separated from my favorite teacher, Mrs. Brown, and my stepbrothers and stepsisters. We all knew each other. I felt safe. I didn't know these new people with whom my father was sending me to live. It didn't matter if they were kin. They were strangers to me.

My stepsister, Audrey Bailey, was in the twelfth grade attending R. R. Morton High School at the time of the school closings. Her class was the last class to graduate from the high school before being closed and padlocked. Later as adults, we talked about it, and I got her thoughts on the school closings that impacted both of our lives. She said that her class was called to an assembly, and they were told that their class would be the last class to graduate because the schools were closing. She said that no one knew how to react. Still, she was thankful that she was able to graduate and felt sorry for those who did not.

It wasn't long after schools closed that my sister, brother and I left Meherrin in Prince Edwards County, Virginia, a place that I define as the epiphany of the African proverb, "It take a village to raise a child." Leaving my whole world behind—teachers, friends, and familiar surroundings—heading off to God-knows-where, I silently cried the entire move. But I couldn't complain. My father wasn't having it. And then, suddenly, a painful shyness began to dwell within me. I was afraid, afraid to speak, afraid to be noticed, afraid to make friends, and afraid to get too close to people for fear we would be separated again. Back in Prince Edwards County, I was comfortable—I had Daddy, Mama, and my siblings. In this new place, I had a few of my siblings, Terrie and Samuel, but no Daddy and no Mama. Everybody knew my name at Levi Elementary School. But, at Abraham Lincoln Middle School in Berkeley, Virginia, I didn't know anyone, nor did I want to get to know anyone and no one seemed to be interested in getting to know this little country girl.

~

A few miles away from Berkeley was Norfolk, which was the big city compared to Prince Edward County. Norfolk had everything a big city offered—bright neon colored flashing lights, plenty of people, plenty of diners, live entertainment, the movie theatre, jukebox music, dancing and mischief. Being a country girl, I wasn't used to streetlights shining in my face and loud talking from crowded streets. I wasn't used to waking up in the morning and eating just cornflakes and milk for breakfast. In the country, for breakfast, we ate bacon, fatback, eggs and homemade biscuit with molasses and plenty of butter. We ate anything fried, from fried white potatoes with onions, fried sweet potato, fried apples, or fried corn right off the husk. I remember Mama making four pans of hot biscuits from scratch. The biscuits would be dripping with hot melted butter. Her recipe was self-rising flour, fresh pork lard (collected from the cooked skins of hogs, after slaughter), and fresh buttermilk. In Norfolk, we were lucky to have enough milk to put in our cornflakes for the entire week. If the milk ran out, we could forget it because Aunt Hattie and Aunt Sadie, my biological mother's sisters, were known to go grocery shopping once a week.

I recall being introduced to Aunt Hattie and Aunt Sadie for the first time. The late August afternoon air was perfect, but the atmosphere in Aunt Hattie's nine-hundred-square-foot apartment wasn't. Both were in their early thirties with soft black curly hair. They were blessed with well-shaped bodies, slightly stocky, rounded off by jutting bottoms. That day they seemed cold, especially Aunt Sadie. Throughout the times I stayed with them; I saw neither one showing any affection to their own children. It didn't mean that they didn't love them in their own way, but just didn't show too many emotions. They weren't huggers, affectionate people like my father and stepmother were. Aunt Hattie did seem nicer than Aunt Sadie, however. Aunt Hattie's arched eyebrows and big brown eyes exemplified her kind nature. During those days, she loved singing, cooking, and dancing. Less than a year after knowing her, she eventually won me over, and I consider her my favorite aunt.

My other aunt, Aunt Sadie, was a cook, entrepreneur, and seamstress—all while holding down two jobs. Everyone in the family had known she would rather be dead than be poor. An impudent woman, she was very bold and sassy, never scared to speak her mind. I had no problems whatsoever in doing what she said, because she intimidated me. A God-fearing woman, who left home at fifteen due to terror and instabilities, she found stability in Norfolk and never looked back.

~

Jean, Samuel, Terrie, and I initially moved into Aunt Hattie's duplex apartment when we first moved to Norfolk. The duplex had two families per unit and was right across the street from other duplexes. When we arrived, Aunt Hattie had her two boys, Bishop and Arthur Lee, living with her. We kids weren't that far apart in age and instantly connected. Her first husband, Alfred Brown, called "Brown," was a successful cabdriver, owning his own cab company. He worked during the day and most nights as well, so we didn't see him much. It took a lot of adjusting the first couple of months, especially after seeing brown bugs running around Aunt Hattie's apartment. I'll never forget when I pointed to one that was running on the kitchen counter.

Auntie Hattie looked at me as if I were culturally deprived. She said, "You never seen a cockroach, child?" I shyly replied, "No, Ma'am," shaking my head at the same time. She told me to get used to them and relieved my anxiety when she said that they wouldn't bite me. Even though she kept the apartment clean, the family that lived beside her was filthy, and their roaches would find their way to her apartment, she explained.

I quickly learned not to lay a sandwich down, because the cockroaches would get a hold of it before I could take my first bite. However, things changed a couple of months into our stay. I remember our excitement when Aunt Hattie left the duplex and moved to a brown-shingled house on Walnut Street in Berkeley. We moved from a cockroach-infested apartment into a place where everything, including the appliances, seemed new. The house had four bedrooms upstairs. It was much different than the duplex. We had a porch and yard with a fence where we could play. I was happier there. It was a step up from where we were. It seemed like we had moved to the suburbs at the time. There were still cockroaches, but not as many.

I remembered Aunt Hattie saying back at the duplex that our roaches came from the filthy people next door. Therefore, I looked judgingly at the individual separate house next door in our new suburban house and wondered how did their cockroaches get way over here to our separate house next door? Did they just walk across the yard to our house? I found myself searching the ground between the houses to see if I saw any cockroaches making their way over to our house. I never did and decided to accept the few we had and tried to keep them under control with Aunt Hattie's usual spray bottle of Raid.

Aunt Hattie, with her outgoing personality, loved to cook. She always cooked for a mass amount of people—perhaps because she had so many people in the house to feed, or maybe because she worked at Gem's Café, a cafe on the other side of town that served white patrons mostly. For years, she was a waitress and cook at that restaurant. She would put just the right amount of seasoning in dishes like corn beef hash and beef brisket that had people coming back for more. Besides cooking, she also took pleasure in helping the less fortunate. Anybody on the block knew that they could come to Aunt Hattie's house and get some food to eat. Aunt Hattie showed her affection in other ways and was a kind and generous giver.

I learned most about giving by watching her and my stepmother. They took such pleasure in helping people. Aunt Hattie was known to let women in need go in her clothes closet, where she kept all kinds of clothes. She had so many clothes that many were on the floor and in piles according to sizes or types. I saw women wipe tears away touched by Aunt Hattie's generosity as they left her home with bags of dresses, slips, undergarments, and stockings.

Just before the end of summer, Aunt Hattie would throw her annual big block party. It definitely was the place to be. She would have the city barricade her street. She had food galore. Most of the food was donated from local businesses. Many local officials, pastors, church members, community leaders, and the community at large would come to meet, discover shared interest and, of course, have fun. Local musical groups performed on a makeshift stage and then when night came, a friend of Aunt Hattie's husband, named Tiko, would turn disc jockey and play popular R&B records of those times. Spinning black vinyl records, he introduced such musical pioneers as Jackie Wilson, The Drifters, Chuck Berry, Aretha Franklin, Tina & Ike Turner, Ray Charles, James Brown, and others to the listening audience.

Making sure everyone was enjoying him or herself, Aunt Hattie would walk around looking stunningly elegant in her fitted skirts and high heel shoes. With the help of her girdle taking care of any little bulges, she had the classic 1950s look of the hourglass shape. Her effervescent personality was very much like that of the late Harlow Fullwood of the Fullwood Foundation. Mr. Fullwood was a kind and respected philanthropist whose foundation gave scholarships to students for college. His annual banquet was also noteworthy. It was indeed the place to be if you liked good food and a wonderful evening listening to music under the stars. It has been said that no one said, "No" to Mr. Fullwood or Aunt Hattie because each had a reputation for doing great things in the community.

Aunt Hattie's husband was a Mason, and she was in the Eastern Star group, a fraternal organization opened to both men and women. As a teenager, through listening to her chats on the phone with folks, I discovered that women must have some affiliation with Masons to join. I recall my father being a Mason and was always sought in the community and at the Masonic Lodge for his bright ideas, support, and help. Aunt Hattie was sought after, too. She took pleasure in helping and attending their charitable events.

I recall watching her dress up in a long gorgeous sequined ball gown for the Eastern Star annual banquet that she and her husband attended. To me, she resembled a movie star when she was all dressed up. I was mesmerized by her dolled-up appearance, watching her paint her lips ruby red and eyelids a glistening shade of brown. At just thirteen years old, she made an unforgettable impression on me. I remember sitting on a stool near her dresser, munching on a Twinkie or whatever sweet treat she had gotten from the bread bakery thrift store, and wishing I was old enough to attend the banquet. Before leaving, Aunt Hattie would scamper across her bedroom wooden floor in red-heeled shoes and then twirl around, her glitter ball gown glistening like the glass of a delicate slipper. "How do I look?" she asked. I would smile and reply, "Beautiful." She'd pat me on top of my head, and then, she and Uncle Brown, in his handsome tuxedo, gloves, and top hat, headed off into the night.

Later, she would come home and tell Jean, Terrie and me about the good time she had. I loved hearing how her night went. Before slipping off her gown, settling in a warm bubble bath and then retiring for the evening, she'd perform some of the dance moves she had performed at the banquet before. She was a wonderful dancer. I supposed that's where I got my love for ballroom dancing and dancing period—either from watching Aunt Hattie dance, watching American Bandstand or listening to records on the jukebox in Aunt Sadie's store.

~

My brother, sister and I didn't know that our stay at Aunt Hattie's would be short. It wasn't long until we moved in with Aunt Sadie who at the time owned her first store called Sadie's & Mike's. I was forced to attend a different middle school due to where she resided.

From the start, I knew Aunt Sadie was a serious person and a strict boss. She rarely smiled. The only times I would see her smile was when one of her sons, Alex "Moses" or Richard "Sidney Poitier" came home from the military to visit, or someone handed her some money. Other than those times, she didn't smile much. I loved her sons. At the time, I considered them my big brothers. Moses was in the Air Force, and Richard was in the Navy and was nicknamed Sidney Poitier because he had facial features like the famous actor. Both men were much nicer than their mother, who worked, went to church, and then went back to work after church. Her store, Sadie's & Mike's, also known as a confectionery back in those days, sold hotdogs with homemade chili, hamburgers, cheeseburgers, French Fries, fried and steamed crabs, fried chicken, and fish. The breakfast menu consisted of egg biscuits, cheese and sausage biscuits and bacon biscuits or sandwiches. In addition, they sold snacks like chips and cheese crackers, canned goods, loaves of bread and other grocery items and household products. I was told later in life that Aunt Sadie sold moonshine in the back room past the kitchen, as well as ran a few numbers on the side.

I don't think we were in Aunt Sadie's house for even a week when I was told to go to the store and work behind the counter, taking orders. At first, I didn't mind because I was older and felt mature as Mama had made me feel in Meherrin. Sadie's & Mike's started out as a fun place to watch black folks eating, playing cards, and listening to the jukebox, dancing, laughing, and essentially enjoying life. But, the second I realized that I couldn't go home when I wanted to leave and had to wait until the store closed, which was past midnight, the work turned from fun to exhausting.

MY BUSINESS ROOTS AND COOKING SKILLS

Looking back, I can see that my experiences at Sadie's & Mike's taught me many lessons that were strictly from Aunt Sadie. She and Mr. Simon, her Jewish friend and store manager, taught me how to run a business, from opening in the morning, cooking, and doing inventory to closing at night. The cooking skills that I had learned from Mama and now her made me the even greater Southern cook that I am today. My family and friends are all in awe of my various dishes and specialty recipes such as my mac and cheese, potato salad, bread pudding, corn pudding, chili, Great Northern Beans, pinto beans, chicken soup, vegetable soup, fried corn, fried apples, and many more dishes.

In fact, my cousin Lorenzo, whom I consider more like a brother than a first cousin, teases me and tells family and friends that I am the only doctor he knows who can cook her behind off. He teases that many of his well-educated friends either don't cook a real meal or can't cook. They usually have just water and rabbit food (vegetables) in their refrigerator. And, they have a plethora of phone numbers for quick delivery of any food one can imagine and can have the food delivered in a flash.

But being the old-fashioned Southern gentleman that he is, carryout is not the same as a good old-fashioned home-cooked meal. His lovely and devoted wife, Bettie, spoils him and often cooks real homemade meals daily as he isn't too keen on leftovers. She, too, is an excellent cook and has added to my repertoire of dishes that I can cook very well. I have a cookbook coming out soon where I share many of my Southern cuisine recipes and healthy-eating recipes as well.

Although I learned several lessons and skills that prepared me for adulthood, living with Aunt Sadie proved difficult at times. She worked me extremely hard while under her care. I was working the hours as an adult before I was legally considered an adult. I thought at the time that it was slave labor. I thought this is so unfair. I mean after school when other school children could rest from a day of classes to go out and play before doing homework, I was behind a store counter taking orders and cooking. I know my textbooks had to smell like a whole lunch. I learned to work expediently, think fast, and count money in my head to give back the correct change, which were skills that I carried with me through life.

I had to remember and internalize what I had read, because I didn't have much time to do my homework. I knew when I got home after working in her store, which many times was after midnight; Aunt Sadie would tell me to turn the lights off, so not to burn much electricity. I had no choice but to study under the covers with a flashlight. And, I better not complain. If I even looked like I was unhappy living with her or working at her store, Aunt Sadie would look at me with those big brown eyes of hers as if to say, "You are a foster child and do as I say. After all, I don't have to keep you. I'm not charging you for food and rent." That was her personality.

MY JEWISH CONNECTION

Aunt Sadie gave Mr. Simon, her Jewish friend, the green light to run her store. To me, Mr. Simon added diversity to the store and gave the business a certain air of respectability. I hate to admit it retrospectively, but he seemed to make it appear legitimate and made it sanctioned as a real business. I must hand it to Aunt Sadie, she knew how to play the business game, and Mr. Simon had the business savvy and an accommodating personality to serve that role. He was a hard worker and seemed to love helping this minority businesswoman succeed.

While working there, I sensed that Mr. Simon felt sorry for me because now and then, he would slip me a few dollars to buy things at school or wherever I wanted just like any other normal teenager. He taught me some Jewish traditions such as the Seder service, and the history of the Holocaust. He taught me how to make Jewish dishes like salmon and rice, brisket and matzah balls, a staple food on Passover. He became a mentor and father figure to me and, because of him I have a special place in my heart for Jewish people. I recall some years later, I was asked by the president of Coppin State University, after being appointed as vice president to represent the college and join the Jewish group called BLEWS, the Black/Jewish Forum of Baltimore, Maryland, which was founded in 1978 as an effort to overcome estrangement between African-Americans and Jews.

I joined and eventually became the organization's vice president for two years and the president the next three years. I was excited to reconnect with my Jewish side of my upbringing. I already had a relationship with this same group of Jewish friends from when I was assistant superintendent of Baltimore City Schools. My area office was in the annex of Pimlico Middle School, which was on the border of the Jewish community when the closing of Pimlico was a hot topic in the black community because of low enrollment. The Jewish leaders attended several community meetings and were most understanding and empathetic to the concerns and helped to keep the school open. I developed many friendships which became helpful in other areas of my life; for example, having my Jewish friend, Larry Stappler, to become Chair of Coppin Foundation Board and to assist with fundraising. Some joined my Coppin State University board and were instrumental in helping Coppin in other ways when I became vice president and president of BLEWS. Many of whom I have met along the way in other capacities are good friends even today.

Another example of my Jewish connection and friendship was when I met Mary Ann Sack through Jeff Donohoe, my Leadership Montgomery 2004 classmate who helped in the planning of the third boys group home. Mary and I connected immediately.

She was a member of the WHCT (Washington Hebrew Congregation Temple) and introduced me to Rabbi Lustig and other ladies of the Sisterhood auxiliary. Under the leadership of Rabbi Lustig and several other female Rabbi leaderships, the WHCT also became supporters, adopted Aunt Hattie's Place and encouraged their synagogue to assist. Mary Ann had a huge fundraiser at her home and invited one hundred of her closest friends in July, when many people are away on vacation. I was so impressed by the turnout. Another Leadership Montgomery graduate and a good friend of Jeff's, named Greg Dillon of Dillon Development Partners went with me to answer the technical questions. Because of Mary Ann's influence, she had a huge crowd who wanted to hear about my vision to discuss the program and the plans for the Sandy Spring new boys' home.

Later that year, I was asked to be the speaker at WHCT's MLK Memorial Dinner. I took a total of eighteen boys from both group boys' homes. And, they were dressed in shirts and ties. The boys did their signature Martin Luther King, Jr.'s, "I Have a Dream" speech and blew the congregation away, including me. Every year since, we have been invited back to the MLK Memorial Dinner as well as their Seder Services.

My foster sons and I enjoy the connection to and camaraderie with my Jewish people. All of this stems from Mr. Simon's kindness in my teenage years. He found favor in me and told me I had a good business head on my shoulder and that I was going to make it big one day.

FINDING MYSELF AND MY PASSION

In Norfolk, I took my education seriously, because I didn't want to be stuck living with Aunt Sadie for the rest of my life, stuck in her store dealing with customers who constantly came in while I was trying to do my homework between customers. There was never any down time in that store. Mr. Simon, sensing my frustration, would often let me excuse myself to a small room in the back with a lamp and allow me to get some studying done when Aunt Sadie was on an errand or off to a meeting. I found favor with Mr. Simon, and I kept in touch with him for years after I got married and left Aunt Sadie's.

Aunt Sadie was a great contrast to my stepmother who seemed to be a happy person, and it made everyone around her happy. While living with Aunt Sadie, I missed the special moments with my stepmother. Although I was angry with my Mama for hiding the fact that she wasn't my biological mother, I missed her warm smile and affection. I used to enjoy that private time in the morning when everyone in our cozy whitewashed house was asleep and it was just the two of us in the kitchen cooking breakfast for the rest of the family. We had that mother–daughter bond. She'd be talking to me, praising me on how well I had set the table, thanking me for doing a great job. She'd say you did that so well, even though I had done it countless times. I love that feeling I got when she praised me or was nice to me. And Mama was always nice to me. Aunt Sadie wasn't.

One day while washing dishes, I looked out the window and saw my father walking towards the house. I dropped the pot that I was washing and ran for the door. I couldn't run to the door fast enough. My brother and sister were already there. When the door opened, we bolted to my father and attached on to him like blood-sucking ticks to skin. We had our arms around his waist and hugged him as tight as we could. Aunt Sadie was sitting in the corner folding clothes with this mean and surprised look on her face as if knowing something was up for my father to appear out of the blue.

Unbeknownst to even me, my sister and brother had gotten in contact with my father either by phone or through mail pleading for him to come get them out of this god-awful place. They were tired of Aunt Sadie's demanding ways. While Samuel and Terrie were talking to my father, Aunt Sadie pulled me to the side and told me that it would be in my best interest for education's sake, to stay with her and let them go back to Maryland where my father had moved the rest of the family from Meherrin.

She knew that I took my schooling to heart and that I felt education held the keys to success, connections and an opportunity to become that teacher Mrs. Brown said I would be one day. So that afternoon, I watched my brother and sister leave with my father. It didn't take them long to pack because I think they were already semi-packed just waiting for him to appear.

On that cold November day, I made the decision to stay with Aunt Sadie to pursue my education. The honeymoon period didn't last long as I had to endure her mean, intimidating and moody personality. Often, I would escape the repressive environment and think back to Meherrin. Oh, how badly I missed the country. I missed the open space and beautiful landscape. I missed the long country dirt roads. I missed hearing the roosters crowing, the cows mooing and the pigs grunting.

~

Several times while working in Aunt Sadie's store, I would go into a trance recalling the day I stayed home from school in Meherrin. It was the day Mama grabbed me in her arms and hugged me and smothered my face with kisses. I had made her so proud that particular day. I was eleven at the time. All the other children were at school. Mama thought I was too sick to go to school that day. She made me stay home. I saw her roll up her hair in pin curls with bobby pins then tie a pretty scarf around her head.

Although Mama was a housewife for most of the time, she would work many days in my father's little store in Meherrin, which was opened for lunch to serve mainly his employees. On this morning, she was headed to the pickle factory about five miles away from our house. She made it a part-time job during the warmer months. She would bring some rejected pickles home for us to eat, but to me her homemade pickles were sweet and spicy and tasted better than those briny-tasting pickles from the pickle factory.

When she left, I was all alone in an empty house. I lay in bed looking up at the ceiling. I didn't feel sick at all that day, so I slid out of bed, pinned my hair up in a scarf like Mama had done, went downstairs, and then peeped out our living room window. It was a gorgeous day. Sunny days in the country were always good laundry days because you could hang up the wash on the clothesline to dry. During those days, washing sheets and clothes was an all-day affair, called "Wash Day." Many steps went into washing clothes on Wash Day.

First, Mama would check the rain barrels that were used to collect rainwater running down off the tin roof of our house to see how much water was available to give to our livestock. If there were any left, she'd use that water to wash colored clothes. Wash Day also required that my siblings and I walk several times to the creek, which was about two miles one way, and bring back buckets of water for the wash. I would watch as Mama and my older siblings would make a fire around a big black pot with kindling and other dry logs to heat the water that we brought back from the creek.

Back in those days, going "green" was not an option. It was a necessity. The hot water would go into our dasher and wringer washing machine my father purchased from Sears and Roebuck. Sheets were washed first with the dasher turning clockwise 180 degrees and then quickly counterclockwise at 180 degrees. After about twenty minutes or whenever Mama thought the sheets were clean, she would strategically put them through the wringer and out the other side, right into a big silver galvanized tin tub that held another two buckets of cold clear creek water. Mama would add bluing, an old-fashioned household product that was once a staple of the laundry room, to the water to make the water a deep blue color.

I discovered later in life why Mama used bluing in the rinse water. It was to make the sheets and white clothes appear whiter. That was very important to rural folks who hung their clothes on clotheslines. They didn't want neighbors to see dingy-looking sheets or white clothes on the clothesline. They took great pride in the whiteness of their clothes. Color clothes weren't that important, but white clothes stood out.

On this sunny day, I did all the laundry and cooking by myself. I walked to the creek three or four times, gathering the water needed for the wash. I poured the creek water and Tide laundry detergent into the black iron pot outdoors and formed a fire to heat the water and Tide. After the Tide had dissolved in the hot water, I filled the washer with both then I started the dashers rotating. Next, I placed the sheets carefully around the dasher in a loose circle. I hand washed a few pieces of whites that had stains with the washboard and then I put those whites in the washer with the other whites.

After washing and rinsing the white clothes in bluing rinse water, I lifted the wet laundry outdoors and placed each piece on the clothesline with wooden clothespins. Our white sheets would blow in the breeze, stretched across our sturdy metal clothesline. I love the smell of fresh sheets off the clothesline. I remember us kids running in between sheets and smelling that fresh scent.

After hanging sheets, I went to our chicken coop. Normally, we waited until evening to catch the chickens because they were less mobile. But, on this day, I knew my family would be hungry after work and school. I wasn't hesitant at all and was quite sure of myself in the kitchen. I approached the chickens quietly and quickly grabbed one caught off guard. I held the chicken close to me, so he wouldn't flap his wings and disturb the other chickens. I did as I had seen Mama do so many times. I quickly spun the chicken in the air by the neck until the neck cracked. I, then, simply pulled the head right off the chicken and let the chicken flap around until he was dead. While that one was flapping, I ran and caught another chicken, who by now knew what the deal was.

We usually needed at least four chickens for each meal. After getting all the chickens I needed, I then tossed the chickens in hot water that was made again in the black iron pot outdoors. After about a minute or so, I removed the chickens and began plucking them one by one to remove the feathers. After the chickens had been plucked clean, I cut the chickens open to remove the guts. Next, I cut each chicken into parts, saving the feet, back and neck for soup.

Then, I seasoned the chickens with salt and pepper just how I saw Mama season chicken in the past. I placed lard in a cast iron skillet and tossed a match on the wood in the stove. I placed the different parts, such as the legs and thighs in a deep bowl of flour. Once the lard turned to hot oil, I dipped the different parts into the hot fat and let them fry, causing the entire house to smell good. Next, I made a big pot of Great Northern beans with chunks of ham hocks, which was the staple of our home. Mama always had a big pot of beans simmering on the stove. On the rare occasions, when she didn't, we had chicken and dumplings, but for the most part, we had beans.

I washed and cut up a cabbage. I added fatback, salt, and pepper to the water and then tossed in the cabbage, placing more wood inside the stove. I knew how my family liked cornbread, so I made a big pan of cornbread to go along with the meal. I used buttermilk and cracklings for the cornbread with plenty of fresh eggs. I got tickled and laughed out loud when I went back out to get the eggs from the chicken coop and saw the chickens scattering at the sight of me as if they thought I was back for another one of them for dinner. Four was enough for today, I quietly reassured them.

I went back indoors and coordinated all the dishes to be ready simultaneously as Mama taught me to do, so everything would be hot when eaten. When the food was almost done, I set the table with our beautiful company china and silverware that we normally used on special occasions. I thought to myself, my family is the company today and after spending the entire day fetching water, washing clothes, running after chickens, and cooking, I wanted them to feel special like company—like the preacher or relatives that came to visit us from the north.

Mama came inside the house and saw all that I had done. Her eyes displayed shock at first then happiness. She hugged me so hard that I could hardly breathe. She was smiling the entire time.

"Sista," she said, "When . . . ? Who . . . ? Did you do all of this by yourself?" I nodded my head with a sheepish grin that was self-satisfying as I said, "Yes, ma'am." Then, she asked me, "How did you know how to do all of this?" to which I replied, "I learned everything by watching you and helping you." She gave me another hug as did my siblings.

That evening I looked around the dinner table and saw everyone eating, rarely placing their forks down. Seeing the smiles on my loved one's faces as they enjoyed a particularly awesome pot of Great Northern Beans, cooked with ham hock, fresh-seasoned crispy fried chicken, well-seasoned cabbage and warm golden-brown cornbread, was love to me. I still cherish that extraordinary feeling of doing something beyond my comfort level to please someone else.

Mama was so proud of me that day that she told anyone who would listen to her story of when I washed the clothes, plucked the chicken and cooked a delicious meal that caused my family to lick their fingers. She even bragged on how well I had cleaned the kitchen when I was done.

Over the years, my cooking skills became better. But I am nothing in the kitchen compared to my stepmother. During those days, people cooked everything from scratch. They were self-taught chefs. I can remember Mama's famous desserts. I loved them all. One being her famous fruitcake—soaked in rum and wrapped in cheesecloth. Mama's fruitcake was the prefect winter treat. There are lots of people out there who don't really care for fruitcake, but Mama's recipe has converted even the most reluctant individuals. Her ingredients were nuts, dark and white raisins, flour, eggs, sugar, and dried fruits such as dates and cherries, and crushed pineapple, cinnamon, nutmeg, and salt. In the back of our house, stood a walnut and pecan tree. During Christmas time, as children, we would gather the nuts that fell on the ground and spread them out on the roof of the shed then crack each nut with a hammer. The nuts were for Mama's famous fruitcakes. Mama always would caution us to be very careful to avoid getting shells in the nuts. She would say, "Getting a piece of shell in your mouth when eating the fruitcake was the worst thing that can happen and will ruin a perfectly great piece of fruitcake."

We children would also help Mama can strawberries, peaches, cherries, and tomatoes. As much as I love to eat fruit fresh, I've learned you can only eat so much on any given day, so I learned to can the rest or make jelly, jam, wine, or freeze fruit. My family loved making our own pickles and particularly loved the unique flavor that allspice, sugar and vinegar added to whatever was pickled. In addition, Mama taught us how to pickle watermelon rind, also known as watermelon pickles. It's a winter treat that I miss dearly.

~

There were so many perks to living in the country—space, quietness, and the beautiful night. Things I miss about living in the country are lightening bugs as a night light, the sun slowly setting on the horizon and the open space. In the country, the entire community would get together and slaughter hogs usually during early winter. The event was called Hog Killing Time. The men would butcher the hogs with big knives and cleavers, and then remove the intestines.

Every part of the pig was eaten from the "rooter to the tooter." The carcasses were cut into hams, bacon, pork chops, pig feet, etc. The intestines, known to many country folks as chitterlings, were a delicacy when cleaned and cooked in vinegar, onions and hot sauce. People who were less fortunate than others loved this time of year because the people from the community would give each other bulks of pork meat to take home.

There was nothing like Mama's crispy crackling to set off a succulent Sunday dinner with her hot savory crackling cornbread with sweet cream fresh butter on top. A Southern staple, I still follow Mama's original crackling cornbread recipe, which calls for fresh, fried pork skins pieces and the grease that came from frying them, coarse cornmeal, self-rising flour, a little baking powder and baking soda, a pinch of salt, and a tablespoon of sugar. I can't forget the buttermilk and the egg slightly beaten before being put in with the rest of the ingredients. I recall, sometimes, Mama would want the spoonbread effect and would add fresh sweet corn to the batter. And, oh! It was just as delicious with the fresh country butter. When I make it, my friends and family lick their fingers just like we did as children.

I recall, Daddy didn't eat the skin on his piece of fatback, and as children, we waited until he had finished eating and left the table before we'd pounce on his plate, eat his skins, and chew on the chicken bones to no end or any other morsel left—including licking his plate—as we were accustomed to licking our own plates.

Mama wasn't the only one who taught me how to cook. My older stepsister, Audrey, taught me how to make fresh coleslaw from fresh cabbage and shredded carrots. I still follow her recipe today.

~

There were moments as children, a few of my siblings and I would get inside or on the back of my father's pickup truck and he would drive us to his lumber business down the dirt road from our house. Many of my father's relatives lived down that dirt road over the railroad tracks where apple trees and peach orchards were on each side of the road. The dirt road was so narrow that we could reach out of the pickup truck and grab a few peaches hanging on the end of the limbs. We'd wave at Aunt Pauline, one of my father's aunts, who was deaf. She nicknamed my brother, Samuel, "Junie Boy." She loved herself some Junie Boy. My brother stayed with her for a while when he was very young after my mother died, and they had become close. Aunt Pauline is no longer living, but I know she would be very proud of my brother today. He received his Doctor of Ministry degree from Union Theological Seminary in May of 2009. Then on September 28, 2014, he became an ordained Bishop.

As children, we would watch all the vehicles and commotion at my father's lumber business. Many, if not most, blacks and some whites alike worked for him. He told us that the men had families, just like him, and they worked hard to provide for their families as he worked hard to provide for us. He said they cut down trees, turning them into lumber. Then they would load the lumber on big trucks and sell the lumber to a sawmill. I saw the long flatbed trucks hauling long lumber logs. I even saw my grandfather, Samuel Neal, known as "Grandpa," by all of us children, working for him. Grandpa had long black hair all the way down his back.

Most of the times, he wore his hair in a long braid with a clothespin or string tied on the end to keep it from unraveling. Grandpa was a very handsome brown-complexion man. I was told that he was part

Cherokee Indian. I remember hearing him talking funny. He had an accent and pronounced his words differently. As children, my siblings and I would imitate how he called certain words. For example, he would say, "It's fuggie, fuggie ut tuday," meaning, "It's foggy, foggy out today." One of his favorite expressions was "It's just like clockwork" to many questions people would ask him. If someone asked him, "How are you today?" He would reply, "Just like clockwork."

I see Grandpa in my daughter, Cheryl, my niece, Michelle, and my granddaughter, Reagan. All three inherited their long wavy black hair and lovely brown complexion from grandpa's side of the family.

~

One would think that a two-room schoolhouse would be crowded. But, when I was seated at my desk at Abraham Lincoln Middle School, that first year separated from my family, I missed the two-room schoolhouse. The school had a small porch in front of each classroom on each side of the building. Levi Elementary School wasn't crowded to me. In fact, it felt like home. I have always appreciated my years there. Levi Elementary will always be special to me for what I discovered there, my inspiring teacher, Mrs. Brown. She was a brown-skin, heavyset, intelligent and pretty woman with what some might call "good hair." Her jet-black hair was wavy and curly and seemed like she didn't have to straighten it with a straightening comb or use a perm. Mrs. Brown taught Pre-K to fourth grade. Including me, she taught about thirty children in total and all of us were in the same classroom.

On the other side of the school, Mr. Johnson, a tall, gray-haired man, who smoked and occasionally would nod off during class, taught grades fifth to seventh. Many times, the mischievous boys, one being my stepbrother, Larry, would skip to the end of the page during reading sessions, while Mr. Johnson was dozing off. They would pretend that they had read the entire page. When the students would laugh, Mr. Johnson would ask, "What's so funny?" to which the boys would say, "Nothing." Mr. Johnson would then say, "Next," meaning the next person to read.

I recalled Mr. Johnson had a white secretion in the corner of his mouth as he talked, and he smelled like tobacco smoke. Nonetheless, he was a nice man who taught his students, English, math, science, and history. During the week, he lived in Grandma Miller's house which was down the road passed our house. Then on weekends he would travel to his home in another part of the state, which apparently was too far to drive every day to teach.

One day in his absence, after devotions, in her pleasant manner, with her pretty flowery clothes and long curly black hair, Mrs. Brown kept the partition up that normally pulled down from the ceiling to create two separate classrooms. She selected me to teach and monitor his class. She told me that she considered me a bright pupil at school. I'll never forget that day, a pivotal moment in time that helped set the contours of my future. She didn't select students who were already in the fifth, sixth, and seventh grades. She selected little ol' me, a fourth-grader, to teach the class.

I sat behind Mr. Johnson's wooden desk and held the class as if I were six feet tall and had been teaching for years. I felt grown and in charge. I was taught well. Mrs. Brown was a great example of how a teacher should be. As I mentioned before, everything I learned as a teacher, I learned from her. I had watched how she orchestrated her time, how she orchestrated peer teaching, and how she orchestrated different subjects going on at the same time. I loved education, reading and learning, two fundamentals that inspired me to teach special education.

At one point during the day the kids were goofing off, one being my stepbrother, Larry. Mrs. Brown's warm, lovely smile turned into a pout. She looked over at me and said, "Sista, what should we do with students who misbehave in class?" Just like my stepmother, Mrs. Brown always addressed me as Sista, and I loved hearing the word

"Sista" part from her lips. I shrugged both my shoulders, caught off guard by her question. She said, "I recommend a switch or paddle to their hand."

I looked over at my stepbrother whose eyes were wide like two silver quarters. Mrs. Brown saw that he was scared, too. She went over to him and the other students who were being disruptive. She bent over Larry and told him if he didn't settle down, he'd feel her paddle against his hand. Larry quickly straightened up. He got off easy that day. But I knew if Mrs. Brown notified our parents of his behavior, Larry would surely receive a spanking when he got home. He was the type of child that just couldn't sit still. The spanking wouldn't be long, however.

Larry was known to get a thin switch and break it slightly, so when my father slapped it against his brown legs, the switch would break in half and the spanking would end fairly quickly because he knew Mama or Daddy wouldn't send him to get another one. Larry told us kids that we needed to follow suit, so that our behinds and legs wouldn't have to endure the slashing long. We thought Larry was a brave soul, and no one else had that much nerve or boldness to try that stunt, but him. I suppose since he was the one getting most of the spankings, for some infraction or another, that he had it all figured out.

VEGETABLE SOUP DAY AND HOMEMADE ICE CREAM AT LEVI ELEMENTARY SCHOOL

Often, Mrs. Brown would prepare homemade vegetable soup on the potbelly stove in our classroom. We were all told the day before to bring a bowl and spoon, as well as a jar of a vegetable ingredient for the big pot of soup. The older students took turns stirring the big pot of hot soup as it cooked and simmered on the stove. They also kept the fire in the stove blazing by feeding the potbelly stove with wood stacked in the corner. Families of students would send wood to school that day because they knew we would be using more wood than usual as we cooked the homemade soup that day.

How excited I was to smell the aroma of the various ingredients—onions, diced potatoes, and tomatoes—that Mrs. Brown would strategically put in later to keep the soup from becoming mush. The meat in the soup was usually a combination of a large hambone and chicken parts like the necks, back, feet, and wings. I remember Mrs. Brown putting the meats on the stove first. When the meats were close to done, she would let the students put in what we brought from home. The hardest part was waiting for the soup to cook and then cool. The delicious aroma in the air caused my stomach to growl and my mouth to water. When she announced that the soup was done, we would line up with our bowls. Mrs. Brown would lovingly dip in the pot of rich vegetable soup and bring out a nice dipper of soup for each bowl, being careful to ensure that each student's bowl had a nice balance of vegetable, broth, and meat.

Later that day, she made homemade ice cream from fresh milk, sugar, and vanilla flavoring. All the students took turns turning the wheel on the old fashion ice cream maker that required rock salt and dry ice. After our tiny stomachs were full, she would read inspiring poems by Langston Hughes and Maya Angelou, Kahlil Gibran, and other noted poets.

Those were the things I missed about Mrs. Brown and Levi Elementary School.

~

During the summer of 1962, I took the Greyhound bus to New York City to visit a cousin, Richard, his wife, Dee, and their three children. This was my first-time visiting New York. Richard was a building manager (called "the super") in a fancy Jewish apartment building in a nice area in the Bronx. He exposed me to a culture much different than Virginia. When I first arrived, I understood why they called New York City a Melting Pot. It truly is a melting pot of different cultures combined into one large cosmopolitan city. I could smell the garlic from the delicatessen. I could go an entire block, and the foods would be different.

During the World's Fair, Richard would take his family and me to Coney Island to go sightseeing. We would go to the beach and walk down the boardwalk where I first heard the song Under the Boardwalk, record by the Drifters. I was a teenager back then, so I loved the amusement park on Coney Island and riding the Ferris wheel and roller coasters and eating my first bag of cotton candy. I also ate my first pizza at Coney Island. I can't say enough good things about New York pizza. My first pizza was fresh, sizzling hot from the oven. It was covered with mozzarella cheese and plenty of pepperoni. The cook drizzled olive oil on top of the pizza, placed it on wax paper and handed it to me. The slice was hot in my hand. Anxious to take a bite, I burned the tip of my tongue, but this was the best pizza.

Several times throughout my visit, Richard would take me to the famous Apollo Theater located in Harlem. My favorite part of the Apollo show was seeing famous musicians like Lena Horne, Sam Cooke, Gladys Knight & The Pips, and Nancy Wilson perform. I would be in awe of their performances. Apollo is hands-down one of the best places to experience in New York.

~

When returning to Norfolk, my happy spirit would turn gloomy. I felt so unloved and unappreciated while living under Aunt Sadie's roof. I probably wouldn't have graduated from high school if it were not for a kind older gentleman named Southall Bass. He served as a freelance photographer at my junior high school and high school. He wore glasses that looked like they were made for his face. He found favor with me. When we first met, he took a liking to me in a fatherly, nurturing way. It was his caring that transformed me from an unnoticed quiet junior high school student to a person who received her high school diploma with honors. He was my surrogate father when my real father wasn't around to guide me on the right path. Mr. Southall Bass noticed me with my head down most of the time walking the halls at school. I'll never forget when I sat in front of his camera to take school pictures. During the session, he was trying to get me to smile for the photo. I didn't feel like I had anything to smile about. I was depressed, angry and most of all, hurt.

Aunt Sadie, a woman who was always critical of things, worked me hard to earn my keep. If I was reading a textbook or just looked like I was doing something beneficial to my well-being, she would interrupt me to go get her a glass of water or fix her something to eat. She could be five feet away from the kitchen, but that didn't matter.

~

Mr. Bass was part of a Christian organization called The Bachelor Benedict Social Club, which sponsored me as a debutante. The organization consisted of successful blacks, like lawyers, doctors, teachers and other professionals. My pastor's son, Vernon, was my escort to the debutante ball. Prior to the ball, we both took dance lessons, learning dances like the waltz, fox trot, and cha cha. I felt like Cinderella that night.

And just like the story of Cinderella, that night ended, and I was back at Aunt Sadie's house mopping the floors and working behind the counter at her confectionary store.

During the week of high school graduation, I decided not to attend. Someone sent word of my disappearance. The police came looking for me. Suddenly, it became very important that I finished high school and participated in graduation. I was skeptical, however. Aunt Sadie didn't seem to care. She never attended any of my school functions. I eventually graduated from high school in June of 1965, and that fall I went to Norfolk Division of Virginia State College, now called Norfolk State University.

The first time I stepped foot on Norfolk State's campus, I was in awe of my surroundings. It was like being in a different world, similar to the then-popular sitcom. I walked inside the main building, called Tidewater Hall then, (now a new 154,000-square-foot building called Brown Hall after George W. C. Brown, one of the founders and first administrator of Norfolk State) and saw a friendly black woman sitting behind the desk. I boldly said, "My name is Hattie Neal, and I would like to know, where is my homeroom?"

She looked at me strangely and rose from her seat. She moved to me and gently grabbed my hand. "Have you been admitted?" she asked. I didn't answer because I didn't know what she meant by *admitted*. I think she could relate to my reaction. She asked, "Have you applied?" Again, I didn't know what she was asking me and just looked at her puzzled.

"You have to register first, young lady," she replied. Then, she took me to the Admission and Registration Office down the hall to fill out the paperwork for admission, as well as financial aid. Being a first-generation college student in my family, I didn't know the process. I just knew I was going to college once I graduated from high school.

One of the admissions and financial aid documents required Aunt Sadie's W2 Form of her income earned. As soon as I got back home and asked Aunt Sadie for it, she yelled, "I don't want them folks in my business!"

Tears began to drop from my eyes, after the verbal slap I had received from Aunt Sadie. She didn't care and went back to doing what she was doing. The next day, I went back to campus. I told them that my aunt wasn't going to give me the necessary paperwork. They told me not to worry and helped me register without Aunt Sadie's W2 Form.

I thank God that He intervened. Because of the trials, setback, and obstacles I have encountered in my adolescent years, I can honestly say that they have made me stronger and more determined and persistent to take negative events in life and turn them into positive lessons learned.

CHAPTER 4

Going Back Home

Seeing the Farmville sign that read Farmville 18, as I approached the city limits, brought back many nostalgic memories of my childhood. My family and I lived in Virginia in the tiny country town of Meherrin in Prince Edward County. Farmville, approximately 26 miles from Meherrin, was the center of attention in the 1950's and '60s due to the civil rights movement. I, along with several of my siblings and stepsiblings, attended school in Green Bay at Levi Elementary School five miles from Meherrin. I discovered during this visit that Levi Elementary School was owned by Levi Baptist Church, according to my interview with Reverend Samuel

Williams, Jr., who served as the Senior Class President in 1951 when Barbara Johns initiated the strike for better facilities at R. R. Moton High School. He was also one of the students, turned plaintiffs, in *Davis v. School Board of Prince Edward County, Virginia*, one of the five cases that were part of *Brown v. Board of Education*. I was excited and anxious to visit my old school while in town and had called ahead and spoken to Ms. Sherre Atkins, Visitor Services Coordinator of the R. R. Moton Museum to tour the museum and have someone to take me to visit my old school for photographs, that is, if the school was still standing. After all, it had been over twenty years since I last visited the school and had someone take a picture of me smiling while standing on the school's steps. At that time, I didn't have access inside the building. During this visit, I wanted to be able to go inside and see the historic two-room schoolhouse that has been such a part of my life memory and the inspirational catalyst for the teacher/professor I am today.

Ms. Atkins arranged for me to meet and interview Reverend J. Samuel Williams, Jr. at the museum as soon as I arrived from Maryland, which was around 2:00 PM. Reverend Williams then arranged the school to be open, so that I could go inside the school.

Once I arrived at the Moton Museum, I looked at the outside of the building and could only imagine the collection of artifacts and historical importance inside. The Moton Museum is a historical landmark located in Farmville, Virginia. The museum attracts thousands of sightseers each year. Both the school and the museum were named after Robert Russa Moton, a celebrated African-American educator and author from central Virginia who was named principal of Tuskegee Institute in 1915 after the death of Dr. Booker T. Washington. Robert Russa Moton held the position for twenty years until retirement. He wrote several articles and books. One being his famous autobiography titled *Finding a Way Out*. Subsequent to my visit, I planned to get copies of the book for Aunt Hattie's Place Summer Reading Program.

I walked inside and introduced myself to the lady sitting behind the information desk and asked for Ms. Sherre Atkins. She lifted her desk phone and called Ms. Sherre Atkins. It wasn't long until Ms. Atkins stepped into the vestibule. She was smiling and told me that she was delighted to meet me. We hugged. Then, a tall man came in behind her with an extended hand. I shook his hand, while at the same time, Ms. Atkins introduced him as Robert "Bob" Hamlin, the Museum Docent. She also stated that he was a student involved back then with the R. R. Moton strike. We all chatted for a moment. Reverend J. Samuel Williams, Jr., walked in minutes later and introduced himself. I was thrilled to meet him. He is a kind, dynamic man with a gentle spirit.

Since Ms. Atkins was working, she had to get back to her coordinating duties, so she couldn't tour with us. Therefore, Reverend Williams and I walked through the beautiful museum viewing pictures on the wall of times past with Bob Hamlin leading the way. Both kind and remarkable men explained various nuances that one could miss if they just toured the museum independently. Their wealth of firsthand knowledge of the strike was priceless as they added anecdotes and reflections that were rich and heartfelt.

After the tour, they took me to High Bridge Church to see an "outhouse" that was still standing in the woods. I was curious to see one. I grew up using an outhouse at home as well as at Levi Elementary School. Back then outhouses were used as the outside toilets. This old outhouse was a wooden structure that leaned slightly to the left. I laughed while viewing it. I couldn't imagine having to use one today. But as a child, I had no choice, until I left the Prince Edward County area for Norfolk, Virginia, when the schools closed. In Norfolk, my Aunt Hattie and Aunt Sadie both had indoor plumbing. To this day, my daughters find it hard to believe that I actually used an outhouse bathroom. I told them that they were fortunate to be born during a time when indoor toilets were ordinary and not the exception to the rule.

After the view of the outhouse, Reverend Williams took me to see the old home place of Robert Russa Moton, which now serves as a hunting lodge. While accompanying me on the tour that weekend, I had an opportunity to interview him extensively. He shared many personal stories, experiences, involvements and his history of civil rights. He even mentioned knowing my pastor's father when they were in Lynchburg, Virginia. Reverend Williams has even done a revival for my father's church, Forest Baptist Church in Meherrin. He indicated that he had met my present pastor, Reverend Haywood A. Robinson III, when he was a young boy, whom Reverend Williams said was talented at an early age. During the interview, Reverend Williams indicated that the high school was named after Robert Russa Moton largely because of Martha E. Forrester, a noted community leader and respected social activist. She named the school after Robert Russa Moton because of his pristine reputation. Therefore, he felt I would want to see Robert Russa Moton's home and take a photo of it as well. I did just that.

~

Later that evening, members of my family met at The Hampton Inn for Meet and Greet over heavy hors d'oeuvres. There, I saw many family members of blood kin or by marriage kin. Estelle Winkler McCormick from Maryland acquainted me with the younger relatives and the ones by marriage.

My most prominent childhood friend and cousin-in-law was Rebecca "Beck" Lee, now Rebecca Lee Randolph. Her father, Edward Lee, was the brother of my stepmother's late husband with whom three sons were born. It was pleasurable and emotional all at the same time to see her after so many years. She was about my age and her older and younger sisters, were close to my sisters, Jean and Terrie's age. I had a wonderful time recapping our heydays. Beck volunteered to take me back to my old home site and to other familiar village sites, houses, roads, railroad tracks, etc., after our homecoming family reunion picnic on Saturday. I was quite anxious to recall my memories of my humble beginnings.

Later, I checked into the Hampton Inn, called my daughters, unpacked, and then retired for the night. On Saturday morning, Reverend Williams offered to take me to Prince Edward Lake, now called Twin Lakes State Park. Before our 1:00 PM reunion picnic, I not only wanted to see where my Levi Elementary School enjoyed our annual field trip outings, but also to meet the homecoming reunion preacher for the reunion service the next day. Reverend Jerry Streat of the Poplar Lawn Baptist Church of Blackstone, Virginia and his congregation had arrived a day early and were enjoying a cookout themselves at the beautiful lake. Reverend Streat was a relative who also was from Prince Edward County and had attended Levi Elementary School. Some of his family members also attended the R. R. Moton High School before it closed.

First, I went to visit the picnic area where as a child I fondly remembered the picnics that my elementary school hosted there. Back in those days, there was about forty kids playing everywhere around the lake and having a blast. My elementary school provided the food, bats, balls, jump ropes, and hula hoops. There were grills for our hotdogs and hamburgers and long picnic tables. I took a short stroll down to the edge of the lake and viewed the quality of the surroundings. The sun sparkled across the water. The scenery resembled a beautiful painting and just like 58 years ago, the area provided a relaxing ambiance just right for picnicking. It seemed as if it were yesterday that blacks were not allowed to enjoy the full range of these beautiful surroundings because there were two sections of Prince Edward Lake, one for blacks and the other section, across the lake, for whites.

Later, a few family members and I went inside the one-story building thirty feet from the lake. A care supervisor walked toward us and introduced himself as Leonard. He was a Caucasian gentleman who looked to be in his late fifties. He took time and showed us around and explained the photos on the wall of various noted black employees and community leaders. I looked at the picture, soaking in memories of a time that is still in the core of my soul. The memories resurrected were joyful realizing how much things had changed at this very lake. Not only did the name change, but also the park is now fully integrated. An hour later, we rejoined Reverend Jerry Streat and members of his church. They were having an incredible time enjoying every home-cooked dish imaginable. I didn't want to spoil my appetite for our family picnic back at our church, so I did a tasting of various dishes. I wasn't disappointed. The dishes I tasted were delicious.

We left the lake and arrived at Levi Elementary School and Levi Baptist Church for our homecoming reunion picnic celebration. I met numerous relatives and friends there that I had not seen in almost six decades. I saw a nice, charming lady who used to straighten my hair and offer positive words of wisdom when I was a young girl. I saw many relatives, relatives-in-law, and old friends. A couple of hours later, most family members and guests toured the historic Levi Elementary School. I looked around thinking how dreamlike this seemed, but at the same time I celebrated the years I had spent in this two-room schoolhouse. Viewing the inside brought back to me so many fond and salient memories. It had been over 58 years since I set foot inside my classroom.

~

My last days at this school were in 1959, when I was passed to the sixth grade at the end of that year. There have been some renovations and alterations to the building, such as the porch where Mrs. Brown used to sit outdoors on her side of the schoolhouse, is no longer a porch. It has been converted to a kitchen, and the pull-down accordion boards that used to separate the two classrooms have been removed to make the building a permanent large room. The large tall windows have been reduced to a regular sized window with plywood, and the chalkboards have been removed and replaced with plywood that has been painted white. The potbellied stoves, one for each side of the schoolhouse, have been removed. The holes for the old stove chimneys were now covered with plywood.

Nevertheless, I could still recall great teaching, learning, cultural enrichment, songs, 4-H Club activities, reading groups, students helping students, writing on the chalkboard, making the fire in the stoves, warming our lunch on the stove, smelling the wax paper in which our sandwiches were wrapped; making homemade soup, recess, May Day festivities, Easter egg hunts in the woods and in the graveyard near the church, dodgeball, hopscotch, ringing of the bell when recess was over, and older boys walking to the Green Bay store to buy treats for the teachers and students. Mr. Johnson would always have the older boys to bring him sardines, crackers and a Royal Crown RC Cola.

Photos were taken of the interior and the exterior of the Levi Elementary School by me and a professional photographer. As I took the pictures, I thought of my two granddaughters, Cameron and Reagan. I personally think I captured the essence of the school. I wanted to show my granddaughters the school that made me want to be a teacher.

After the family reunion picnic, I followed Beck back to Meherrin, which was about five miles away. We drove down the road where I used to live with the fifteen of us in that one house, some of whom were my step and half siblings, and I would get lost in the shuffle. My formative years were spent in that one house from about age three to age ten. My mind went back to the aroma of Mama's fried chicken and homemade biscuits. I remembered how we would change out of our school clothes and go do all the things children do—play in the yard, climb trees, go swimming in the creek. My siblings and I had a good time just being children.

Beck and I turned onto the road off Route 360 Hwy where we used to catch the yellow school bus that Mr. Miller, the bus driver, drove. Mr. Miller was a jolly old man who didn't take any slack from us school kids. He was nice, but if you were out of line, he'd not only threatened to kick you off the school bus, but notify your parents, too. And, if you missed the bus, Mr. Miller would wait for you for so many minutes. If he didn't see you, he would leave. If you missed the bus, you might as well start walking to school, because there was no going back home. Beck and I laughed, recalling how many times my sister, Jean, and some of the older kids, had missed the bus. We calculated how far to Levi Elementary School from the bus stop. The school was almost four miles. They had some walking to do.

Later, we drove to a road named Mill Creek Road, instead of Route 662, which I remember. In fact, all the roads in Prince Edward County have been renamed, and the street names are named after the names of the families that lived or still reside on those streets. Beck told me that individuals suggested to the county what they wanted a street name to officially be renamed. She also enlightened me of Prince Edward County Courthouse's first black female Clerk of the Circuit Court, Machelle J. Epps. This fact was not only shared by Beck, but also mentioned again by both Reverend Williams and Bob Hamlin later. A very proud accomplishment in this small niche black community.

Beck proceeded with our memory-lane tour, and then she took me past the house at the corner of Mill Creek Road and the road that led to my old home. There was a wooden old, dark house on the corner. I remember this was the corner house where Jack, the spotted dog, would lay waiting for my sister, Jean, who normally arrived late to the bus stop. I smiled as I recalled the fear Jean had of Jack. Jean hated that dog with a passion.

Mr. Dawson, a nice old man who was in his eighties when I was a young girl, lived in a small wooden tin-roof house. I noticed his house was no longer there. Beck told me his house had been torn down and a new house was constructed a year and half ago. It wasn't long until a black middle-aged man walked out of the house and sat on the porch and observed us as we took photos and chatted about our past. Beck pointed with her head and said, "That's the person who lives there now."

I smiled at him and explained who I was and why I was taking photos of the street signs and that corner. He smiled and wished me much success.

Before evening arrived, we drove our cars down the road toward my old home site, but could only go so far down, roughly about two city blocks due to the erosion and unevenness of the terrain. Therefore, we stopped the cars at the fork in the road—one road going to the right to the back of our house and another road going to the left around another way to the front of our house. We stepped out of our cars and walked the rest of the way down the right side of the road to where my house sat. I was very excited, reminiscing as Beck and I talked and walked on that brushy-grown road toward my old house. But, to my great disappointment, there was no sign that my house was ever there.

Suddenly, I became emotional that my house was no longer there, as the tears welled up in my eyes. I felt as if there was no proof of my memory and of the happy times I enjoyed in this same clearing when I was a child. After all, it has been over fifty-five years ago. Another house had been placed on the parcel of land as well as a trailer nearby. Despite my disappointment, I took photos of the location and tried to deduce where my old house used to be located and where the sheds, chicken houses, smokehouse, outhouse, truck sheds, and other landmarks of times past were located, too. Then, my eyes suddenly grew wide. There it was! I spotted the covered well. After sighting the well, my perspective became clear as I could now imagine where all the structures were, using the well as my point of reference.

After several long minutes just standing there and soaking in the memories, Beck and I talked about how her mother would walk down the road, many days, to our house. Her mother would come to visit my stepmother and while her mother and my stepmother talked, Beck and I played in the woods games like hide and seek and hop scotch. We laughed when we talked about Aunt Mary, who we lovingly called "Fat Mary" behind her back, of course, because she was a bit on the chubby side. Aunt Mary was a dear relative of my stepmother, and she would get together with my stepmother and Beck's mother and make quilts.

Beck and I then recalled the starch our older sisters would use for their can-can slips to put under their long flair skirts to make their skirts stand out when they walked with their "squeeze-me-tight" wide stretch belt. Being the younger sisters, we always looked up to our older sisters and wanted to be them.

Later, we walked back up the road toward our cars. As we walked, we searched for landmarks to see if we could recognize where my house was. We tried to envision where the front porch and the hedges that were at the edge of the front yard were—not far from the road that went around to the front of the house and led to Grandma Turner's house. Grandma Turner was related to my stepmother and her house was about half a mile down the road past our house.

I tried to locate the tractor loader that my father used to load tractors on his flat-bed trucks, but there was no sign of the tractor loader through the woods or anywhere near. We walked and looked through the woods thinking we could find it. We figured that the new owners had removed it or had torn it down with all the other dwellings.

A couple of feet away from our cars, we stopped on the side of the road and reminisced about when our mothers talked about more serious matters, such as integration, the R. R. Moton Strike, and how the NAACP and others played a vital road in ending segregation. We remembered those meetings and talks back then but was too young to fully understand what was happening and how the impact of that part of history would affect us years later.

Rebecca and I walked to our cars. We got inside and had to back our cars to Mill Creek Road at the corner. We stopped, got out of our cars, again and took another picture of the new sign that now read Mill Creek Road. I said jokingly, "If my father still lived here when the road's names changed, our road probably would have been called "Neal Creek" after my father Samuel Neal. Beck laughed out loud.

About an hour into our journey, Beck drove me to Baileys Road. She pointed to where the sheriff now lives, an African-American man named Stokes. She smiled while telling me that the majority of the people in town were happy and privileged to have him as sheriff, especially knowing the history of racism and segregation in this county.

As we continued the tour, I noticed a house with a pile of wood on the porch. I took a picture of the house because it reminded me vividly of our old house and the piles of wood that my older brothers cut up to heat the house. Mama also needed the wood to cook our meals. I remember back then; we had several large neat piles of wood outdoors in different places on our property and even piles under the house. There were piles of wood indoors as well—a pile in the kitchen by the stove, a pile in the hallway by the heater, that warmed that part of the house with the heat traveling up the stairs to heat the upstairs, and a pile of wood in my parents' bedroom.

My parents' bedroom was where, as a family, we would gather and sit around the pot-bellied stove in the evenings and play creative games during the winter months. Daddy or Mama would send sticks of wood to our school for the pot-bellied stove to heat our two classrooms. Since my father was in the lumber business, once a year, he would bring a truckload of wood to the school, and the big boys would stack the wood neatly, bringing some inside and stacking it against the wall and the rest outdoors was stacked on the side of the school building.

After leaving Baileys Road, I told Rebecca that I wanted to tour Campbell, a small community named after a prominent family. As we rode through Campbell, several new houses were now on that road which has been renamed Campbell Crossing Road. We saw the railroad tracks and reminisced about the two train tracks—one going north and one going south. I remember, as children, we could hear the train coming and could see it far in the distance, although there was no Crossing Bar that would drop down to stop from crossing the tracks. You just had to Stop, Look, and Listen before you crossed the tracks.

~

Later, Beck and I drove about a quarter of a mile up Highway 360 to see the store to which my brothers and other older students would walk and get snacks and treats for us younger students and the teachers. The store is now an empty building. After taking a picture of that old store, Beck and I just walked around the front of the store, stood and talked and reminisced about the fun we had as children. This was such an emotional yet fulfilling moment that seemed to touch the depth of my soul in a woebegone moment, yet in an everlasting way. After almost 56 years since I left the security of this small close-knit county where everyone knew everyone's name and felt like family, I felt sad, feeling that this would be my last time walking in my past life and in my childhood footprints. These footprints had so many pleasant memories at a time of innocence before we knew the impact that the landmark case of desegregation would have on us and our future struggles thereafter.

After settling down our emotions, we hugged and said our goodbyes and looked forward to seeing each other again at church the next day for the homecoming reunion service. I drove my car back to the Hampton Inn in Farmville. Reverend Samuel Williams was riding with me during most of the tour and provided additional stories and anecdotes. During our ride back to his car, he talked at length about more history of the community, various laudable persons in the community and the importance of the R. R. Moton strike that led to the various civil right cases. He told me he had pastored the Levi Baptist Church, and then left to become the pastor of another church in the south. And later, he returned to Levi Baptist Church to be the pastor again. He confessed that the Levi Baptist Church was like coming home; because this was where he was during the time he was involved with the strike. As well, he was a plaintiff in the landmark case. I thoroughly enjoyed my time interviewing him. After obtaining such rich and resourceful information from both Beck and the tour with Reverend Williams, I was feeling energized and nostalgic though tired from the long day. I went back to the hotel to write notes, call my daughters and foster boys and get ready for our reunion homecoming service at Levi Baptist Church the next day.

~

The following morning, I arrived at church early and was greeted by various family members and other family-like people in the community whom I remembered. Back then, we called them "Aunts" and "Uncles"—not knowing then that some of them were not biological kin. There were numerous commemorations in the church's windows of families that apparently were donors and part of the church renovations, which consisted of a new dining hall built onto the church. The beautiful dining hall allowed members to have their cookouts and picnics in the spacious and air-conditioned facility. Prior to the renovations, the church had its annual homecoming gatherings outdoors under the tall shady trees in the back of the church.

I was handed a program by a friendly usher. I looked at it and was quite moved. The reunion program itself was quite extensive and had a lovely church on the front that resembled the old church before renovations. I took a picture of the front of the program as well as the inside to commemorate this wonderful homecoming family reunion weekend.

Reverend Barbara Reed opened the Praise and Worship part of the service. The Praise and Worship service was so spiritually uplifting, heartfelt and inspiring, especially when a kind gentleman named Herbert Lee got up and testified about the importance of family, memories, and friends. It was very powerful and touching as he talked about the true meaning of family. At the end of his testimony, he leaned over in the microphone and said, "It is a blessing to have such an awesome family."

Everyone in the church stood to their feet and gave a heartwarming round of applause.

I looked around the filled church. I felt the same excitement of

Christmas, seeing the various family members who had comeback home from across the country, as well as members of the community.

After Praise and Worship, Reverend Williams welcomed everybody and introduced the preacher for the homecoming reunion service, Reverend Jerry Streat from the Poplar Lawn Baptist Church in Blackstone, Virginia. He was the reverend I had seen yesterday enjoying a picnic at the lake with a group of his church members. It was terrific to see him again after so many years.

When Reverend Streat preached, he was most inspiring, enthusiastic, and just an outstanding man of God. It was rewarding to hear him and to know that God is working in his life. Not only was his sermon phenomenal, but also his choir was phenomenal and the songs they sang stirred everyone spiritually. The young man on the drums was an incredibly, talented young man. There was an older gentleman in the quartet who had a spiritual aura about him. He reminded me of my cousin, Lorenzo, who sang in a quartet called the Silver Trumpeteers years ago. Then there were the pianist, the choir director, and the choir. All of them were in sync as they coordinated together, harmonized and expressed their love for God. There was not a dry eye to be found in this soul-stirring rocking country church on Levi Road.

After the captivating sermon by Reverend Streat, Reverend Williams called me up to say a few words. He mentioned to everyone that I had attended the two-room schoolhouse next door and that I was writing a book.

I stepped onto the podium and as I opened my mouth to speak, I became so emotional. I saw a beautiful sight—the many faces of family and friends. After controlling my emotions, I paused for a few seconds and indicated how I so wish they could see what I saw from my vantage point—that is, this beautiful family. I thanked everyone for coming. I commended the planning committees for a superb and well-planned picnic, the day before; and expressed my pride in the maintenance of the Levi School in addition to the lovely renovated church. I encouraged the young people to be all that they can be in life and to share the rich history of this area with the world. I told them that we were part of a national phenomenal—*Brown v. the Board of Education*. And, that landmark case is part of Prince Edward County's legacy. I encouraged everyone to appreciate our very own family members in this church, other community leaders and descendants of the civil rights era that took place right here in our county that made a national impact.

I told them that I was afraid that the next generation of our children may not know of the trials our forefathers endured and the sacrifices they had made. Therefore, I encouraged everyone to take their grandchildren and other relatives and friends to visit the Moton Museum to learn of our history and its impact on the world as well as help fund the museum so that our history and our legacy can survive for generations. I also challenged the family and the church members to make the Levi Elementary School a historic landmark. I told them that there are not too many one-room or two-room schoolhouses left. I emphasized how it is crucial to preserve Levi Elementary School, in addition to the Moton Museum, because if not, we may lose a generation of kids who do not understand how that two-room schoolhouse play a significant part in history.

After my remarks, everyone applauded. I thanked them and returned to my seat. I was filled with so much joy and love. I couldn't stop the tears from falling. I discreetly wiped them away. The wonderful choir sang another beautiful emotive song that touched my heart even more. The medley played in my head long after the service was over. After a delicious meal in the new dining hall, we said our goodbyes and gave repeated hugs and kisses. We pledged to continue coming to future homecomings. I passed out my business cards and brochures, got some emails and phone numbers from various people. I commended the reunion coordinators for doing a stellar job. Both ladies smiled and thanked me for coming.

Beck and I went to visit my cousin, Linwood Johns and his wife, Sylvia, down this rough terrain of a road to find these lovely homes in the clearing once down this seemingly forsaken dirt and gravel road. I met Dan, another sheriff, who is married to Linwood's niece.

Later, the sun was settling on the horizon. Beck and I thought we had better tackle that treacherous rough road while it was still partially daylight because driving country roads would've been even more of a challenge in the dark. We said goodnight and reconfirmed our plan to meet at the Moton Museum the next day, as I wanted them to tour this breathtaking and memorable museum. After arriving back out to the main road, Beck went to the left, back to Meherrin and I went to right, toward Keysville. I was told by Linwood and Dan to take that route back to Farmville that had more lights and less chance to run into a deer.

I put the hotel address in my GPS and approximately thirty minutes later, I arrived back safely at my hotel. Before settling in for the night, I looked over the museum books and other materials I had purchased. A wealth of history was inside each book. I would share these books with my foster boys and granddaughters, when I saw them. I believe young black Americans need to know it hadn't always been easy for blacks in the United States. Schools were very different, when I was their age. Although things have drastically changed, many civil rights activists sacrificed their lives for a better tomorrow.

The next day, I spent the early part of the day at the Farmville courthouse to check on property that my father owned and to see if the taxes had been paid and by whom. I received copies of the various transactions of my father's property for the last thirty years. The ladies in the office were most helpful and friendly. One of the ladies was very interested in my story of my involvement with the school closings in 1959. She even offered to send me more research materials for my book after I returned to Maryland.

That morning, I met Linwood, Sylvia, and their son, Donovan, at the museum. They had already seen the Barbara Johns' movie when I arrived. Sherre Atkins, the museum coordinator was off on Monday.

So, she had arranged for Shirley Eanes and Brenda, two tour guides, to show us around the museum. They were very instrumental in setting up the opportunity to meet Joy Cabarrus Speakes, one of the original R. R. Moton strikers. The plan was to meet her at Applebee's where we were to have lunch later. It wasn't long until Reverend Williams arrived at the museum. We toured the museum with Sylvia, Linwood and their son. Sylvia and Linwood were astonished at the impact that their relative, Barbara Johns, had on this community. They didn't know there was so much history in the museum about their relatives, Vernon and Barbara Johns.

Around 2:00 PM, we all gathered at Applebee's where Joy Cabarrus Speakes and some of her friends from out of town were already seated at a table. I was in awe to meet her. She talked about some of her experiences back during the strike in 1951. I knew I wanted to interview her more extensively before I left town and made a tentative arrangement to do so either that evening or the next morning. She told us about Barbara Johns' gravesite at Triumph Baptist Church, in Darlington Heights, roughly eight miles from where we were. She also mentioned that a road marker of Vernon Johns was a half a mile down the road from the church to commemorate and pay tribute to his historic contribution to this community.

Because I didn't want to pass up the opportunity to see these historic markings, Reverend Williams agreed to lead us to those sites. After lunch, we rode to Triumph Baptist Church. We took pictures of the church and walked over to Barbara Johns' gravesite. I took pictures of Barbara Johns' headstone and of other familiar names, such as the Gaines, the Watsons, the Holcombs, and the Stokes.

Tears left my eyes. Because of people like Barbara Johns', doors became open for black Americans. She was quite vocal in her opposition and it paid off. She is greatly respected in Prince Edward County and throughout the country.

Later, we stopped at Vernon Johns' marker, which was also in Darlington Heights. I took pictures of his marker, in addition, to pictures of Linwood and his family standing beside the marker. It was because of Vernon Johns' connection with the NAACP; he worked hard in the fight to desegregate schools.

Upon leaving the gravesites, I said goodbye to Sylvia, Linwood and Donovan. All three were headed back to Meherrin. Reverend Williams and I rode back to the museum and toured it again. Afterward, I called Joy Cabarrus Speakes and asked her if I could interview her that Tuesday morning. She gladly obliged.

The next morning, Tuesday, July 22nd, I met with Joy for the interview (see transcription of interview with Joy). As we talked, she thought it would be an awesome opportunity for me to also meet and interview Edwilda Allen, another original striker of 1951. I told her that I would be honored. She therefore called Edwilda who readily agreed to come. She lived just across the street from the museum.

It was noteworthy getting an opportunity to interview these significant icons, who are part of the history of Prince Edward County, which led to the *Brown v. Board of Education*. What united all the strikers I spoke with was a sense of having been so utterly transformed by their experiences who had become educators and spokespersons on behalf of the civil rights movement.

~

Interview Of Joy Cabarrus Speakes—Original Striker; Plaintiff For **Davis v. School Board of Prince Edward County, VA and Development Chair of the Moton Family Challenge—At the Robert Russa Moton Museum on July 22, 2014**

www.motonmuseum.org

Hattie: I'm Hattie Washington and this is Tuesday, July 22, 2014. I'm here at the R. R. Moton Museum. I'm very fortunate to have Joy Cabarrus Speakes who is one of the original strikers in 1951 at R. R. Moton High School in Farmville, Virginia. So, thank you for taking the time to come interview with me. First, could you share with me who you are and what you were doing back in 1951 to become one of the Strikers?

Joy: Good Morning and thank you, Dr. Washington for giving me this opportunity. I attended R. R. Moton High School from 1951–1955 and was a freshman when the strike occurred on April 23, 1951. I was one of the over 400 students that walked out on that day.

We were attending the all-black school, R. R. Moton HS [Robert Russa Moton High School], a school built in 1939 by Martha E. Forrester; a capacity of 180 students. The school is now the Moton Museum, a National Landmark. We are sitting in the auditorium which is now Gallery one of the Museum.

At the time that we went on strike, there were over 400 students attending the school. We were attending classes under inferior conditions and in tarpaper shacks that had been built. The tarpaper shacks were heated by wood stoves. Some students had to keep their coats on in the winter because it was so cold; others that sat near the stove had to take their coats off because it was too hot. The roofs leaked so you had to put up an umbrella when it rained. In the auditorium there would be teachers sitting on both sides teaching classes. We did not have a cafeteria or gym and the biology class had only one piece of equipment.

We would test and dissect frogs as best as we could. The white school [Farmville High School], which was a couple of blocks away, had a cafeteria; it had a teachers' lounge; they had a gymnasium, lab, and athletic field. They had all these amenities and we had none. Our parents had been attending the PTA meetings repeatedly asking repeatedly for better conditions: A new school, and each time they were turned down.

Hattie: Who were they asking?

Joy: They were asking Mr. McIlwaine, the superintendent of schools, the school board and they asked the Board of Supervisors for appropriations so we could get a better school. That did not happen. We had second-hand buses and sometimes we had to leave school early because of the shortage of buses.

Barbara, at one point, talked to her music teacher, Mrs. Davenport, and expressed to her the frustrations and dissatisfaction with the conditions we were subjected to in order to get an education.

Mrs. Davenport said to Barbara, "Well, do something about it." At the time, Barbara thought that Mrs. Davenport was just brushing her off. What Mrs. Davenport meant was that if you want to improve the conditions then you should do something about it.

Our teachers, even though the conditions under which they had to teach were bad, were excellent teachers. They gave one hundred and ten percent [110%] to us getting a good education. They would say to us, "What college are you going to attend? What do you want to be?" They were just expecting us to go to college.

Our parents were disciplinarians; so were our teachers and our principal, Boyd Jones. They wanted us to be well prepared for the future. Barbara decided to do something about the conditions. She secretly formed a committee, which no one knew anything about, except the ones she trusted and had assigned to the committee to prepare to go on strike.

About a month before the strike, there was a bus accident in Prospect, Virginia, a place called Elam, and five students were killed on the bus. One of the students killed was Barbara's best friend. That encouraged her even more that something had to be done. That happened in March 1951 and we went on strike April 23, 1951.

Hattie: What grade was she in at the time?

Joy: Barbara was a junior.

Hattie: Ninth grade?

Joy: No, eleventh grade. I was in the eighth grade when we went on strike.

Hattie: R. R. Moton went from the eighth grade to the twelfth grade? And she was in the eleventh grade?

Joy: Yes. On April 23, we went to school, and it was school as usual. We did not know that Barbara had organized the strike to take place that day and had appointed someone to get the principal away from the school.

Hattie: The Principal then was M. Boyd Jones?

Joy: Yes, M. Boyd Jones was the principal and Barbara had John Watson leave the school to make the phone call to Mr. Jones.

Hattie: What was his position? Was he a student?

Joy: Yes, he was a student also; he was on the planning committee. John [Watson] made the call to the principal, pretending that he was a business man in Farmville calling to say that there were students down at the train station creating a problem and he needed to come down there immediately.

Mr. Jones went because he didn't want any of his students downtown in Farmville misbehaving. There were others posted along the way so when he left, John gave a message to the others, saying that he had made the call and that the coast was clear, Principal Jones had left the school. When he did that, Barbara sent a note signed with the initials BJ to all the teachers asking them to come to the auditorium. Barbara Johns and Principal Boyd Jones had the same initials, so the teachers automatically thought that the principal was summoning everyone to the auditorium.

When we got to the auditorium and the curtains on the stage were opened; it was not the principal. It was Barbara standing on stage. This was shocking to everyone. Barbara asked all the teachers to leave. There were a couple of the teachers who didn't want to leave and had to be escorted out.

Hattie: By whom? The students?

Joy: Yes.

Hattie: They had to be escorted out?

Joy: Right. Barbara wanted them to leave because she did not want them to get in trouble. She said, you could lose your job and we don't want the county to feel that you were involved; that you were the ones who influenced us to go on strike. After all the teachers were out of the auditorium, she gave her powerful speech. I was sitting right over there [*pointing to the very spot in the Moton Museum that is still the original auditorium*] and her sister, Joan, was sitting three seats in front of me. Every time Barbara said something, Joan slid farther down in her seat [*chuckle*] because she feared what her sister was going to say next.

Her speech was inspirational. Barbara just had the persona that when she spoke you listened. And, she could inspire you to do what you needed to do. Just looking at her from day to day you wouldn't think that she had that in her, but her brother said that she bossed them around at home. Barbara was the oldest; her mother worked in DC and she oversaw her siblings.

Barbara's speech ended with all the students leaving the auditorium to go on strike. Some of us went home when we left the building, and some went downtown in front of the courthouse and to Mr. McIlwaine's office. Barbara and Carrie Stokes wrote a letter to the NAACP asking them to come to Farmville to help us. Oliver Hill and Spotswood Robinson came to Farmville for a meeting and the rest is history. We, along with four other states (Washington, DC, South Carolina, Delaware, and Topeka, Kansas) became a part of the *Brown v. Board of Education* landmark decision on May 17, 1954.

Shortly after the strike Barbara was sent to Montgomery, Alabama to live with her uncle, Vernon Johns, because there was fear for her life; that she would be hurt or killed. Barbara died in 1991.

Hattie: Thank you so very much, Joy, for sharing your firsthand knowledge and experience with me for my book. Your interview has been most informative and memorable and an honor for me to be able to interview an icon and original striker of 1951. Thanks.

Joy: My pleasure, indeed. I enjoy sharing the rich history of Farmville and Prince Edward County that also contributed to national history in the landmark case *Brown v. Board of Education,* Topeka, Kansas. The *Davis v. School Board of Prince Edward County, VA* was the only student-led case, where I was a plaintiff; and over 70% of the plaintiffs in the *Brown v. Board of Education* case were from Farmville.

Hattie: That is noteworthy, indeed. Thanks again.

~

Interview of Edwilda Allen—An Original Striker of the R. R. Moton High School Strike in 1951 at the R. R. Moton Museum in Farmville, VA, July 22, 2014

Hattie: This is Hattie Washington. This is July 22, 2014, and we are now talking to the infamous Edwilda Allen, who was one of the original strikers back in 1951.

Well, thank you for coming up. This is beautiful, and I'm not going to keep you long. Tell me a little about your recollections and your reflections of the strike briefly and how you were involved with the strike.

Edwilda: Well, Barbara's sister, Joan, and I were in the same grade. And, she was a year younger than the rest of us. Sometimes in those days if you had a whole bunch of children you sort of got that last one out early.

Hattie: I was one of those children also because I couldn't go to school until I was seven because my birthday is in October. So, I was in school with the younger people.

Edwilda: They hadn't strictly put those rules out there yet. And, she was a year younger than I was and she was crying. I just decided that I was grown up and took her under my wing. She laughs now and says, "You were in first grade and I was in first grade—because we didn't have kindergarten." And, I said, "Hey little girl, what's the matter with you?" And, we just got to be friends through that.

She lived in a rural area and we were friends all the way through it; because if we had a dance at school or something she would come and stay with me so that she could go to the dance and other kinds of activities. And, when we graduated and we went into the world, I was getting ready to get married. I said, well, I want Joan to be in my wedding, and she called me back and said, "I'm getting married the same day". So, neither one of us could be in each other's wedding. We've been friends ever since.

Hattie: Where is she now?

Edwilda: She's in New Jersey, East Orange maybe. Because a lot of folks I went to school with went that way. Either New Jersey or Baltimore.

Hattie: But in 1951 when Barbara did the strike how were you involved with the strike?

Edwilda: Well, she needed people to tell the students what was going to happen and not to tell their parents. That was the big thing! And, she knew me; so, she just picked me to tell the eighth-graders what the deal was.

Hattie: And what did you tell them?

Edwilda: I told them that the bell was going to ring and that they should get up and walk out of class; and if the teachers tell you to come back you just keep on going. That was the biggest thing. Being disobedient was something unheard of. My mother worked in the school district and she was what you'd call a Jeanes supervisor. And, what she would do is go out to the schools and see if they had things in order and how to organize.

Hattie: Did she come out to Levi—The two-room schoolhouse?

Edwilda: I'm sure she did. But then when the walkout started, they [The School District Administrators] tried to find out who started it. And, when they found out I was involved in it [the strike], she lost her job. I really don't know what happened, because from what I remembered she couldn't teach anywhere in the State of Virginia; so, she went to North Carolina and she got a job. She would come home on Friday and go back to North Carolina on Sunday. I was in College when she got a job again in Virginia. I went to school in Wisconsin and went to work in New York. Then, I ended up getting married and going to California; and I didn't come back here until about 1988.

Hattie: And why did you come back [to Farmville]?

Edwilda: I came back to bring my daughter to Longwood College. My sister taught at Longwood.

Hattie: Is she still there?

Edwilda: No, she's retired now. She came back [to Farmville], and my daughter didn't want to go to the school [college] in California. I don't know why, but my sister said she could come stay with me here and go to Longwood. She said that would be okay. So, I came back here to bring her because she's a vet, and we had to travel with a dog. We had gone to the airport right before she was supposed to fly back here, and we had found this dead dog in a cage at the airport. And, she said, "Mom I can't put him on the plane."

I said, "Well, I've got to hose him off, and we'll just drive back"; and that's what we did. I think it was 12:30 PM when I pulled up in my mom's driveway [in Farmville], and the car just stopped. And, I couldn't even jumpstart it. That's how I ended up back here. I still knew some people here who asked me if I need a job. I said, "Yeah, I need a job." And, I started teaching at Prince Edward High School.

Hattie: In 1988? Elementary or middle school or high school?

Edwilda: Yes, well, actually I'm a music major so I was going to work all three schools. Anyway, when they finally read my paperwork, they found out I could do things other than music; so, I was being thrown around all over the place.

Hattie: They were trying to utilize your many skills?

Edwilda: Yes, I could also speak Spanish because you know in LA [Los Angeles] there were a lot of Spanish speakers.

Hattie: So how did you get into music down here?

Edwilda: Well, my father insisted that we play. We started taking lessons when we were six. We had a piano, and he was determined that we were going to play. His mother played. So, we didn't have a choice. We outgrew the Black teachers. My daddy was good at playing "Stepin Fetchit," and he went over to Longwood to find out if there was anybody who would take two black girls. And we found Mr. Alfred Strick, who came from New York. What we did was climb through the window to get into his studio. And Daddy stood outside to watch and made sure that nobody was watching us.

They eventually found out that we were taking lessons over there and threatened him [the music teacher] so he had us come to his house. He was the one that kept us on target. Since I had so much music, I couldn't quite decide [in college] because I also wanted to be a doctor. But I didn't want to give up all my music. My mom started doing some research, and we found out about music therapy where you would work with those who are mentally ill or physically ill.

And, at that time, there were only three colleges in the country that had majors in music therapy. There was Boston Conservatory, the College of Pacific and Averno in Milwaukee [WI], which is where I went because I figured it was the closest. My daddy didn't want it so much because it was a Catholic school, and he thought I would become a nun. They [the Catholic school] only had six black girls, and I was the only non-Catholic student in the school. Since I was in music, I sang in the choir and learned to play all instruments.

Hattie: Tell me about the busing situation and how you got to school.

Edwilda: The kids who lived in the rural area rode buses; however, the black children who lived in town walked from their house to the black school in town. When they got to be in eighth grade, all black children had to come to Farmville to go to the one black high school in the county that went from eighth grade to twelfth. There were five high schools in the county for white children. When the Board of Supervisors decided to close the public schools, Mr. Fuqua gave the money to build five private high schools for white children—one school per five magisterial districts.

Hattie: Yeah, we went back up to Green Bay. Mr. Miller was our bus driver. After picking us up at the fork in the road, he went on up [the road—Route 360] and picked up the Winklers and the Bookers. I don't know how he ended up back here [at the Levi School in Green Bay]. I think there was a street that came back around [Lutheran] because I don't remember him coming back down that same road [Route 360] to get to Levi. But if you missed the bus, you walked [to school] through what we called Campbell [now called Campbell Crossing].

Do you remember "Beck" [for Rebecca] Lee? She took me all through there [Campbell Crossing] on Sunday [July 20, 2014] after church. I lived down here from age three until age twelve. Then, my father sent the four of us, my biological brother and two sisters, to Norfolk. And he still stayed down here for a while—because he had married Hilda Lee [Neal], and she had six kids already, three Bailey's and three Lee's. My father's last name was Neal [Samuel Neal, Jr.]. They then had five kids together by the time I was 12 and had to leave for Norfolk.

Edwilda, what would you want to share with people about all your experiences with the strike and the whole civil rights movement back then, especially with children in schools today, etc.?

Edwilda: I lived in the place where everything was segregated, but I think my mother and father did a good job of explaining things. Our backyard was here [*pointing on the table as a diagram*] and the white family was here, and they used to climb over the fence and play with us. I can remember the day when he [a white kid] came and said, "I'm going to go to school, and my daddy said I can't play with you anymore." I told him, "Well, my daddy told me that a long time ago." So, segregation was all around you, but I think our parents did a good job of helping us to deal with it.

One minute, the white children would come over to the house to play and eat, and then suddenly, they don't talk to you anymore. So, when things happened, it didn't take long, I just bounced out of it, and went on dealing with it. I lived across the street from the white elementary school. It was all brick, and steamed heat, so you could see the differences; you didn't have to have anyone tell you anything. We walked to school, but there was a bus that came in front of my house every day and picked up the white children. So, I saw the bus filled with white children every day, while I was hiking up the hills for about two miles to go to my black school when there was a white elementary across the street from my house and a white high school four blocks away. So, the things that might have bothered somebody else, I knew about. I just dealt with it [the reality of racism]. We got see racism firsthand daily as the white students would laugh and throw things such as bits of food, fruit pits or anything else they had to throw from their bus window daily.

Hattie: You just accept it [the reality of racism] as it was, and didn't know if you could change it or not, just accept it?

Edwilda: Well, so when Barbara [Johns] came and said to me that you know how our school is and how their [the white students'] school looks, it wasn't new or shocking because we lived it every day. And, the crazy thing was she wanted me to meet her down on the athletic field—meaning I would have to cut class. My mother and father were going to kill me. That's all I could think about.

But I respected her because she was the oldest child in her family; and her mother and father worked in Washington, DC, and Barbara and her sister, Joan lived with their grandmother. I always knew she was very mature and very grown up for her age. So, when she asked me to do something, I said, "Okay." Then, I said, "What?" She then went on to explain the other reasons for her plan. Because I thought all I had to do was whisper in somebody's ear and tell them to go and do something, that wasn't [going to be] a problem.

Hattie: I guess back then it was daunting for students to take the lead like that?

Edwilda: Yeah, it was. You didn't go against what adults were telling you to do, even if you didn't believe what they told you to do, you just didn't go against it. My daddy was an electrician, and we lived in a time when people in the rural areas didn't have electricity. So, he would go, and they were beginning to bring the electric lines through. He would go and wire people's houses. Because I said I used to go and run into people down there and they would say, "Oh, your daddy brought us lights, I know your daddy." So, doing something against what I was supposed to be doing was . . . but I said "Okay" to her [Barbara Johns].

Hattie: What was so interesting was the idea of children taking a stand, because in all the other cases, it was adults who took the lead in those cases. Topeka, Kansas, South Carolina, Delaware, but to have this, Prince Edward County, to have students to do that is, to me, astounding!

Edwilda: Yeah, even though they told us not to say anything, I went home and told my daddy what was going to happen. And, he just looked at me and said, "Well?"

Hattie: Now she [Barbara Johns] told you this on that day before it was going to happen?

Edwilda: No, I knew a couple of days before it happened; I don't remember the exact day. But, after she told me separately, she told me to meet her down on the athletic field. There were some other people down there already. First, she said I need you to meet me down there at such-and-such time on such-and-such day. Now, they [The Prince Edward Board of Education] were building temporary buildings all around, more than six buildings. There were rooms out here [*pointing in the direction of one street*], then one big room for the agriculture people there. And, then, there was one on this street. I guess there was one here [*pointing outside from where we were sitting in the auditorium*].

So, you know, you walked through this building here [*pointing to the R. R. Moton building where we sat for the interview*], and around, depending on how long you want to take to get to class. And the teachers had to move too. They had to move with all their books in their arms, moving from classrooms to classroom.

Very few teachers had a personal or permanent room; Like the Home-Ec [Home Economics] teacher did because it had the sewing machines and stove [in that classroom] and the librarian. But everybody else [all other teachers] just moved at the same time [as the students].

Hattie: Isn't that amazing? That is amazing! Well, I have taken up enough of your time. I really appreciate it so much.

Edwilda: Oh, you are so very welcome. It was my pleasure. Take care of yourself, and I would be anxious to see the book when it is finished. Good luck!

CHAPTER 5

Raising the Bar:
Rearing My Daughters to Become Professional Women

What would life be if we had no courage to attempt anything?
– VINCENT VAN GOGH

"Is there a doctor in the house?" When asked this question by a reporter once, I answer with pride and thankfulness, "Yes! There are three: My older daughter, Charrell Washington Thomas is an M.D [Medical Doctor]." I was equally as proud and grateful to inform them, "My younger daughter, Cheryl Washington, is a J.D. [Doctor of Jurisprudence, an attorney], and I am a Ph.D. [Doctor of Philosophy]."

Ever since I was a little girl, I have been motivated and driven to succeed at all costs. I learned early to stay focused, work hard, and pursue my dreams, regardless of the sacrifices needed and the roadblocks encountered. Therefore, I didn't expect any less of my two daughters, even though they grew up in a time when expectations of and opportunities for girls were sometimes not equal to those for boys.

My mantra is: *Don't tell your daughters to marry a doctor or a lawyer. Tell your daughters to be one.* As a proud parent, I consider myself blessed for accomplishing an undertaking that has proven both challenging and rewarding. With the help and favor of the good Lord, I raised two African-American daughters to be the first doctor and the first lawyer in our family, and they have more than exceeded my expectations. I was blessed to have beautiful, smart and talented little girls; from birth throughout their childhood and teenage years. I taught them that beauty came from within and that good manners and a pleasant personality will get you much farther in life than physical beauty and even brains.

I taught my daughters not to internalize another person's negative judgment or negative view of them and end up developing low self-esteem that could affect them in related ways. I know firsthand how people can misjudge you or not like you for no known reason that you can discern other than racism or some other characteristic such as your parents' occupation, where you live, or even how you look.

Growing up in Norfolk in my teen years during desegregation, I experienced some of these same unfair judgments by society in school and in life, so I taught my daughters how to anticipate and handle such issues of unfairness when they most assuredly would encounter. God directed my path and protected me from developing low self-esteem by filling my path with numerous mentors.

Being an educator and parent, I share with parents that it's crucial to start early and let your children, especially girls, know who they are as an individual and to be self-assured enough to be bold and stand up for what's right, even if you are standing alone. My advice also to parents is to give your children boundaries. If there aren't any boundaries, your child won't know the difference between right and wrong. But, when there are rules, they will know the difference. Or, they will know when they have broken a rule or have deviated from the expectation. When your child does well, you want to praise him or her. Through praise, you encourage them to continue doing well.

Also, parents are to set the example. Believe it or not, you are your child's role model. If they hear you using profanity, then they feel it's acceptable to use those same words at school or elsewhere. If they see you stealing, in their mind, it's okay to steal. If they see you driving and texting or talking on the phone, they think its fine to do so as well, even though it's against the law. What can we say to them? We've got to set the example.

There were rules in our home by which Charrell and Cheryl were expected to abide, as well as any of their friends who visited or called the house. For example, when my daughters' friends called the house, they had to show respect and use good manners, or my daughters would not be allowed to take the call. I would tell their friends how to communicate respectfully and effectively when they called my daughters—not to call there without speaking and just ask, "Is Cheryl home?" I would ask very emphatically, "Who is this?" to which I would get his or her name. Then I would say, "If you ever call here again, your first words should be, 'Good evening, Mrs. Washington'; identify yourself and say, 'This is Tyrone', and ask politely, 'May I speak to Charrell or Cheryl, Please?' Got that?"

I usually would get a pause or a "yeah" to which I would respond, "Say, yes ma'am or yes—not yeah." And then, I would say, "Now, let me hear what you will say when you call here again." After their reply, I would say, "Beautiful!" I would then call the girls who were usually cringing close by with embarrassment.

I recalled one day while straightening up Cheryl's room; I noticed several index cards in her dresser drawer. She had written detail instructions for her friends on what to say when they called our house, and I answered the phone. She had on the cards:

"Good evening or Good morning, Mrs. Washington. My name is _____. I am a friend of Cheryl (or Charrell), and I am in her class at school or on her team. May I speak to Cheryl (or Charrell), please?"

I read each card, and they were all the same as if they were business cards that people hand out to other people. Apparently, she made it quite clear to anyone she gave her phone number how to call her house. I realized that was why all her friends knew what to say and how to call them at home. I got so tickled and laughed out loud and thought, bless her heart, how ingenious. That's my creative, analytical-minded Cheryl. That same social personality caused her to run and win the title of runner-up to Miss Norfolk State, when she was in college.

~

I remember meeting my husband during my eleventh-grade year in high school. He was in the Navy and four years my senior. When in port, he would often stay with one of his navy friend's family members who lived across the street from Aunt Hattie's house. During those days, I was staying with my other aunt, Aunt Sadie, in the suburbs of Lambert's Point and had to catch two buses to get to school. My daily routine after school was to walk from Booker T. Washington High School to Aunt Hattie's house, which wasn't that far from the school. I wouldn't walk alone. Both of my cousins, Barbara and Geraldine, walked with me down the street about three blocks to the bus stop. At the bus stop on Church Street, I would board the bus, heading home and usually get off the bus an hour later, in front of Aunt Sadie's restaurant. I would work in her store until late and then go home and try to do my homework.

I recall one afternoon at the bus stop, upon realizing that the bus was running late; I heard a man say, "Hey, pretty lady." My cousins, Barbara and Geraldine, looked past me. I turned around to see who caught their eye. A tall brown-skinned, handsome man was smiling and looking at me. I caught a whiff of his cologne that smelled expensive. He said, "May I take you out on a date, pretty lady?" I was thinking, *What a predictable line for a sailor and that he has got the wrong lady, mister worldly navy man.* My immediate response was, "No. Thank you." While I had seen this man occasionally across the street, we had never spoken. I didn't know him, and he was much too old for me to date, I thought. He was persistent, though, and asked the question again. I told him any young man I dated, first had to go to church with me. Secretly, that was my way of getting rid of him. But, then, he asked, "Where is your church?" Startled, I told him and thought that would scare this sailor off, and good riddance. Who does he think I am?

But sure enough, he showed up that Sunday dressed in a gray sharkskin suit. He looked rather dapper, I must admit, and was quite the gentleman and the eye catcher of all of my church girlfriends. I later consented to let him take me out on a date, not knowing then that our first date would lead to three years of dating . . . when he was in port. On the third year, he popped the question of marriage to me. After being assured that I could continue with my education, I said, "Yes." There were no objections from my family or his after we told them the news. In fact, Aunt Hattie and Aunt Sadie purchased my wedding dress, and my pastor's wife and other relative and friends decorated the church pink and purple for our wedding. Mr. Southhall Bass took our wedding photos.

We got married when I was in my second year of college as he was about to board a navy ship to go overseas for several months. My senior year in college, I discovered I was pregnant with my first daughter, Charrell. When the doctor told me that I was pregnant, I was both elated and frightened because I didn't know what to expect. I didn't have my own mother nor my stepmom to talk me through the process. I felt alone. My husband was on a navy ship most of the time; therefore, letter writing was our way of communicating. That was before the age of emails, texting, skyping and other social media processes that we have today to communicate. He was delighted to hear the news.

During the latter part of my pregnancy, I was invited to come and stay with my pastor, whom I affectionately called Uncle Herman, and his wife, whom I likewise affectionately called Aunt Helen. They thought a young woman shouldn't be staying in an apartment by herself, especially while pregnant. I took them up on their offer to stay in their guest bedroom. I packed my clothes and belongings and moved from our small furnished apartment in with them. Very pleased with my decision, Uncle Herman, Aunt Helen, and their attentive three children (Vernon, Herman, and cute little Phyllis) were kind and generous, going above and beyond to attend to my every need.

As soon as I settled in, I wanted to get started being a great mother early, so I played soft music just for my baby, while pregnant, and would read to Charrell as if she were already born. I read books to her such as the Bible, Dr. Seuss, Mother Goose and even my college textbooks. I played soft music after reading in one of my college psychology textbooks that pleasant music would create a calm state of relaxation and stimulate a natural tendency for the baby and mother to be emotionally and psychologically healthy and calm.

But delivery day was just the opposite and was very difficult for me. The pain was excruciating and frightening as I didn't have my mother to tell me what to expect with my first birth. It felt as if lightning bolts were striking my stomach.

Once my water broke at my pastor's house one afternoon, while Aunt Helen and the other children were at work and school, the hospital trip was left to nervous Uncle Herman to drive me speedily to Portsmouth Naval Hospital. Although it seemed as if every stoplight would turn red, we finally pulled up to the Emergency Room. With perspiration now dripping down Uncle Herman's face, he sighed and belted out, "Thank You, Lord."

Hospital staff rushed out with a wheelchair to assist me into the delivery room. Moments later, I received a large needle for pain. After numerous pushes and a lot of moaning and groaning, Charrell entered the world. The moment the doctor told me that I had a beautiful, healthy baby girl, tears fell from my eyes. When I held her in my arms, my entire face was soaked. She was the most beautiful baby I had ever seen. Of course, every mother thinks her baby is cute, but when I first laid eyes on my baby, I thought, "Did I produce this Cutie?" She had the prettiest black curly hair and light brown skin. She had my husband's and my father's features. She was a big baby, 8 pounds and 11 ounces.

Charrell was three months old, when her father's ship returned in port at Norfolk Naval Base. She was a wonderful Christmas present, which I dressed in red and white for her first family Christmas cards that I sent to the entire family. My husband was in awe, too, after seeing her. Being home for several months gave us a chance to move into our next apartment and bond more.

I recall dressing Charrell in the cutest baby clothes that I purchased from JCPenny's and Sears. Charrell was an eye-catcher and her friendly and calm personality caused people to gravitate to her. When different ones came to visit, the first thing that would come from their mouths was, "Can I hold her?"

At the time, I was still teaching Sunday School at my church, New Hope Church of God In Christ (COGIC), a church that started with about twenty members and eventually grew to over two thousand members. I had been a Sunday school teacher from eighth grade until I finished college. Church members, friends and family members would put in their bid early to keep Charrell in church while I taught Sunday School, especially the teenage girls. And, I was thankful for the help.

I completed my bachelor's degree in elementary education with an endorsement in special education a few months before Charrell was born. It wasn't long until I was convinced by the principal of Abraham Lincoln School to come teach a special education class. The previous special education teacher walked off the job in the middle of the year because the students not only had learning problems, but also had behavior issues.

I was hesitant at first. Charrell was barely four months old, and I was not comfortable leaving her yet with a babysitter for long periods of time. When I was told that I could bring her with me to school, I accepted the offer to teach that challenging class of students. I would wrap Charrell in a pink blanket and put her in a basinet in the front passenger's seat of my car. And, off we'd go. During those days, you weren't required to place a baby in a car seat on the back seat of the car.

Periodically, I'd look over at Charrell, who would be smiling and waving her little baby hands in the air while I drove us both to school. Once staff and students caught a glimpse of the new baby, they fell in love with her instantly. Various teachers would come to get her and show her off all over the school, making her coo and smile. The students in my class would get jealous and ask, "Where is our baby?" I thought that was too cute. These supposedly hardcore students with behavior problems were talking baby talk to Charrell and worked hard to finish their schoolwork to have extra time to play with "their baby."

Charrell was so well loved in that school.

My second daughter, Cheryl, was born two years later in the same month. And, just like Charrell, she was a gorgeous baby with features of my grandfather—lovely brown complexion with thick jet-black straight and slightly wavy hair. I experienced the same joy after Cheryl's birth as Charrell's, but I was a little confused. I thought I was having a boy. The old folks at church told me that I was having a boy. I heard them say things such as, "You're carrying the baby up high. And you're experiencing heartburn. Oh yeah, that's a boy."

When the doctor told me that the baby was a girl, I lifted my head off the hospital bed and said, "Huh? Are you sure?"

As I looked at her, my reaction changed quickly. I became instantly in love. When I arrived home with Cheryl, I laid her on my bed and went to the back of my closet. I smiled with happiness. All Charrell's baby clothes were packed in boxes. I unpacked each box of these perfectly good clothes, and they were passed down to Cheryl.

Although grown now and a top-notch lawyer, Cheryl is still my baby girl who has always looked up to her big sister. Being only two years apart in age, Charrell and Cheryl were very close growing up and did many activities together, from ballet lessons and piano lessons to girl scouts.

When we lived in Scotland, they went to different British schools, but still found time to play together and read together. They also took piano lessons together, pony trekking, Scottish country dancing, calligraphy, library trips, and joined The British Girl Guides (our Girl Scouts) together.

~

During the years, I learned in order to be a good parent you must manage your emotions and well-being as a new mother who was also a working single mother (sort of as a military wife). You must take care of yourself, so you can take care of your children. My biological mother died when I was two years old, so I wanted to be there for my girls. I practiced good hygiene and nutrition and taught my daughters the same. I committed myself to be the nurturing and compassionate parent that I imagined my mother would have been and wanted for myself. I not only told my children that I loved them, but also, I tried to show them every day with plenty of hugs and kisses and signs of approval.

Research indicates that children who feel loved do better in school and in life. They thrive more in life versus children who don't feel loved and wanted. I also taught my daughters sound principles of reading, spelling, writing, and speaking.

For example, before we ate dinner, they were required to recite a different Bible verse after we said grace, except they could not say a short Bible verse, like "Jesus wept." Because the main goals of this strategy were twofold: That they learn the Bible; and then practice memorizing information, which helped their memory and speaking abilities in school. Some days, before dinner, I would see them scurrying and quickly looking in the Bible for a Bible verse to say at dinner. I would smile to myself and pretend that I didn't see them learning the verse just minutes before dinner.

Before bed, when they were younger, we prayed together and then I would read storybooks to them such as Children's Bible stories, Mother Goose, Dr. Seuss and others. As they got in middle and high school, they read world classic books or other novels from the library and ended the night by listening to tapes of vocabulary words from the series of *3000 Words All Executives Should Know* softly playing in the background. I challenged them to learn fifty of these new words every week; that is, the meaning, the spelling, and how the word is used in a sentence.

Once, Cheryl was complaining about the vocabulary routine and remarked that she and her sister were the only people she knew who had to listen to vocabulary words every night and read at least one book a week and be ready to give me a two-minute synopsis of the book upon request. She said that none of their friends had to do that. To which I responded by saying that I was not their friends' mother, I am their mother. And that I was not trying to be your "friend" right now; I am being your mother. And to trust me, it will pay off one day.

Some years later when Cheryl applied to law school and had to take the LSAT Exam, she confessed to me that the reason she was able to do extremely well on the exam was because it was an analogy-type test, which was mostly vocabulary words. She said if she didn't know the meaning of a certain word, it would have been be more difficult to deduce which was the right related word for the analogy question. She thanked me for making her continue the vocabulary nightly routine and for not allowing her to stop because she didn't like the process. Every parent wants to hear their children tell them later in life, Thanks for being my "Parent" and not just my "friend." Be persistent, consistent and systematic in showing "tough love" to your children regardless of their negative attitude and resistant behavior during their adolescent years.

~

Looking back, feeling unwanted, unloved, and unsupported as a teenager, propelled me as a mother to prepare my daughters academically for the future. Additionally, I strived to attend all their school and extracurricular activities. Although I worked a full-time job, I devoted much time to them. I tried not to miss anything in which they were involved whether it was a play, sports, piano recitals, ballet performances, and other involvements. I even was the president of the Parent–Teacher Association (PTA) the entire time they were in junior high and high school.

I remember those hurtful days when I was in plays, selected to say Hamlet's soliloquy "To be or not to be . . ." and other presentations during my high school years, when I had no one out in the audience supporting me, no family involvement whatsoever. I felt neglected and abandoned. But I had to keep my head up and keep striving through the pain of neglect and abandonment. Tears would fall down my face and at times a caring teacher would ask, "What's the matter?" To which, I would answer, "Nothing!" and kept what was hurting me inside.

After becoming married and having children, I wished I had my mother to be there for me and to offer to help me out, to babysit my children, her grandkids, or do whatever and whenever I needed her.

I felt that my daughters didn't have a real grandmother as they grew up. Yes, my stepmother was living in Baltimore, Maryland. But, for years I harbored resentment towards her for not revealing the truth to me. She wasn't my biological mother and kept that one important fact from me. And then there was Aunt Sadie, who showed me very little affection nor that much to my daughters as compared to how much she showed to her own grandchildren. She'd even charge me to keep my daughters whenever I had to attend a meeting or some other activity and couldn't take them.

Out of courtesy, I offered to pay her; to my chagrin, she would take the money when offered and stash it in her bra. I felt so hurt behind closed doors and like a single parent, since my husband was away in the service much of the time; and his own mother seemed to favor her six other grandsons, by my husband's brother, more than her two granddaughters. I was a military wife with little family support.

As a result, I am the type of grandmother today who hasn't missed a Grandparents' Day since both my granddaughters have been in school. Whenever they participate in a dance program, I'm on the plane headed to Florida. To this day, I make it my duty to attend as many of my granddaughters' school, church, sports and other functions as I humanly can—even if I must fly in for their ten-minute-or-less performance and then fly back out the next day. And yes, I will do that for my adorable granddaughters, Cameron and Reagan. When I see that gleam in my granddaughters' eyes when they see me sitting out in the audience makes it all worth the trip.

Every time I see that gleam in their eyes, I'm reminded of the time when their mother, Charrell, was in medical school in Charlottesville, Virginia and was chosen during choir rehearsal that Saturday to sing lead solo just before the minister preached on that Sunday. I was living in Randallstown, Maryland during the time. Charrell called me that Saturday evening and wanted me there in Charlottesville the next morning to hear her sing her solo. My nostalgic heart would not let me even think of not moving heaven and earth to be there, especially the way she asked with such exuberance and pride. I started out early that Sunday morning and drove the three hours to hear my baby sing her song.

Unexpectedly, traffic caused me to run late, and I thought I had missed her singing. I eventually arrived ten minutes later than planned. However, as soon as I walked in the church, I was ushered to a special seat as if they knew who I was and that I was coming. The song that the choir was singing immediately stopped and her song started to play, as the choir director waved his hands in the air. At that moment, I heard the most beautiful sound coming from off Charrell's lips. I remember thinking, this is perfect timing, and I didn't miss my sweetie pie sing after all. I breathed a sigh of relief. "Thank the Lord!" I shouted my words with gratitude.

After service, the minister whispered in my ear that Charrell told him and the choir director that since I was not there yet, that she could not sing her song until I had gotten there. Therefore, the choir kept singing a song and then another song as they kept a keen eye on the church doors for my arrival. Hearing that story, I hugged the minister and church director and thanked them for being so understanding and gracious. They said that they were just so proud Charrell, this UVA (University of Virginia) medical student, who found time among her studies to join church and sing in the choir; and that they were glad to honor her wish. They applauded me for coming all that way for Charrell's no more than a five-to seven-minute solo. If they only knew the significance of seeing that gleam in her eyes, just seeing me sitting there while she performed, meant to me. I had to be there for her.

A MOTHER'S LOVE

For most of my earlier childhood in Meherrin, I thought my family was perfect like the 70s television series *The Waltons*. I was treated very well. I felt safe and most of all, loved. But there was a period in my teenage and adult life when I didn't talk to my stepmother. She and my father eventually left Virginia and moved to Maryland, but soon after the move, they divorced. She lived with some of her older children in a legendary Baltimore City row house with marble steps.

I knew where she lived. My father told me where she lived. He would go visit to drop off the child support checks. He told me he and my stepmother would often sit on the marble steps and chat about Virginia and the impact the school closings had on families, including ours.

Although they remained cordial, I refused to visit her, as I was still angry with her. My mind kept revisiting the moment when my father told me that she wasn't my biological mother but was my stepmother. Then if that weren't enough, I was given away to be raised by a strange woman who was mean and didn't try to show love. I was snatched from my sanctuary and was left to travel alone in this world. That experience hurt me to my core. It was a deep wound that wasn't healed. I had felt that my entire childhood was a total lie.

Then one Christmas day, after visiting my father in Baltimore, I decided to drive to my stepmother's house across town. I couldn't stand the separation from Mama any longer. I brought Charrell with me. She was almost a year old. As soon as I stepped inside, my stepmother jumped up from where she was sitting with her usual cup of coffee with plenty of cream and sugar, hugged and kissed me as though I was still her favorite child, and as though I was ten years old again. I sat on her couch and watched as she enjoyed and bounced Charrell up and down on her knee, talking baby talk to her while holding her two little hands.

The words were in me. A single question. I wanted to know the reason she had lied to me all those years. I stood up and moved toward her. I looked at her with the coldest of eyes. I mustered the courage and asked, "Mama, why didn't you tell me you were not my real mother?"

She looked me straight in the eyes seemingly hurt by my question. She came closer, put her hand on my shoulder, as she used to do when I was a little girl, and replied softly and lovingly, "But I was."

For a moment, I didn't understand what she meant by that statement. I was confused. Didn't my father tell us that she was my "stepmother" years ago? Why is she lying to me still? Then, seemingly, the expression on her face said it all. It showed love, hurt, and the years of longing and missing me. The years apart went before my visual imagery like a fast motion picture showing me all the good times we had as well as the lonely teenage years being raised without her in my life. Then, I finally understood what she meant by her answer, "But I was" to my big question.

The anger and resentment were replaced with shame, guilt and humility after hearing those words part from her lips. I started crying because I finally got it. All those years I had played the victim role. All those years I had wasted when she felt that she was my "real mother." And, truthfully, she was the only real mother that I ever had. Deep down, I knew it.

She kissed me on my teary cheeks and the pain of deception, guilt, and time wasted was replaced with joy and gratitude. She had put it all in proper perspective for me. We hugged for a long while.

That was a very special moment in my life. From that moment, I decided never to let resentment and misunderstanding define my life again.

CHAPTER 6

The Dark Secret

"There are no secrets that time does not reveal."
– JEAN RACINE

While visiting my cousins, Lorenzo and his sister Barbara, in Virginia Beach over the fourth of July weekend, I went to visit my namesake, Aunt Hattie, who is the oldest known member on my biological mother's side of the family. She lives in a lovely house in Norfolk, which is part of a redevelopment plan for the community around Norfolk State University. I was so thrilled about seeing her as it had been a few years since our last encounter in person—though I always sent her a Christmas, Easter and Mother's Day card with a check.

I wanted to ask her questions that would fill in the blanks about my mother, my upbringing and anything she could tell me about any aspect of my childhood, as I was writing my life's story. I went inside her home and noticed her seated in the living room. She was ecstatic to see me and thanked me for taking the time out of my short stay in Norfolk to give her a visit. We hugged tightly, and she kissed me on my cheek, all the while smiling as if I were sunshine on a rainy day and remarking as she looks at me closely, "If you don't look like your mother I will hush."

I got a chair from out of the kitchen and sat next to her, wanting her to recap some family history that she and my Aunt Sadie had been closed lipped about every time one would ask them about their mother and father, my grandparents. I wanted an understanding of our family roots and the sequence of events and places they lived.

After a moment of chatting about my daughters and granddaughters, showing her photos on my iPhone, and indicating how proud I was of them, Aunt Hattie and I began discussing our family tree while sipping on iced sweet tea that she'd made earlier that day in preparation for my visit.

Aunt Hattie indicated that her mother's name was Lina Rosetta Henry Goganious. Her father's name was Walter Henry Goganious. Her parents married in a small church in the town where she grew up. She indicated that her father was part Indian as well as part Greek, given the reason for the unique name "Goganious." He had an accent, but she didn't know the origin of the accent. Aunt Hattie described her father as a brown-skinned man, who was very handsome. She said that my mother and she resembled him.

As my visit continued, Aunt Hattie validated the birth order of her siblings. First came her oldest sibling, Lorenzo Goganious, father to my oldest cousin, Lorenzo Goganious, Jr. Next, there was thick-skinned Aunt Sadie, the aunt I stayed with through high school and the first two years of college. There was my mother, Lucille Goganious, who died when I was three, followed by Aunt Hattie and then Uncle Roy, the youngest.

I had enjoyed the time spent with Aunt Hattie, learning my family's past, but the last hour of my visit was the most intriguing and, yet sad. After heaving tears, she revealed her tragic experience of child abuse. She has been wanting to share family secrets that have been on her mind for years, secrets that have been bottled up only to cause her to have recent nightmares as she turned 90 of incidents as if they had happened the previous day. She looked at me with the saddest eyes and revealed to me that she and her siblings were told by their father never to share the things that went on behind closed doors—whatever went on in their house better stay in their house.

Aunt Hattie finished the last swallow of tea in her glass. I offered to pour her more tea, but she waved her hand dismissively before reaching for a Kleenex on her coffee table. I noticed more tears rushing down her face before she even continued her story, eventually wetting her flowery blouse. She was hurting inside. After getting herself together, she indicated that they lived in Driver, a neighborhood in Suffolk, Virginia. They stayed there until the big secret came to a head by way of a screeching halt. Then, she and her siblings were sent to Wilmington, North Carolina to be closer to her grandmother during the devastating ordeal. Her voice became almost quiet. She lowered her eyes then lifted them and said, "My father, who was your grandfather, was a cruel man. He used to not only beat us children with sticks, branches, cords, or anything he could get into his hands, but also he was cruel to our mother, who was your grandmother."

My heart began pounding with sorrow and anger, after hearing this. Aunt Hattie told me that her father would punch, kick, and slap her mother around, leaving many bruises, welts, swollen eyes and nosebleeds, even blood-stained clothes. If that weren't horrible enough, he would even get his loaded gun and chase their mother through the house all while she and her siblings were yelling and screaming at him not to shoot their mother.

I sat back in my chair in awe. I came searching for answers on my mother's side of the family past and wasn't expecting this. I held my tears, but I wanted to cry because the things Aunt Hattie was telling me were so vile. She told me that her father would then point the gun at them and chase them throughout the house. They scattered and hid deathly afraid, trying not to breathe for fear that he would find them and shoot them. Aunt Hattie told me that sometimes they would hide for what seemed like hours.

My aunt wiped more tears running down her cheeks and then said that it was always their older brother, Lorenzo, who would eventually come out from where they were hiding and let them know the coast was clear. Their father was either routinely drunkenly asleep or had left the house. They would hug each other and go find their mother. When their father was done beating her, sometimes almost to the point of unconsciousness, they would become even further horrified after witnessing her swollen and bruised body. Each sibling would take turns putting salve on her wounds, hugging her and wiping her tears away. They were devastated by the cruelty at the hands of their own father and couldn't understand why and how he could inflict such agony and pain on his family.

More disturbing was how helpless they felt. They were afraid to do anything about it, especially when they were told that this was the family business, and they better not spread family business out in the community.

Therefore, they suffered in silence. Aunt Hattie told me that it was not unusual for them to go to school with welts, bruises, and swollen faces. It was also not unusual to see other children with evidence that they, too, had been whipped. They would simply look at each other with much empathy but wouldn't dare say anything other than what they had been told to say if anyone asked what had happen. "I fell down in the briar patch" or "I was kicked by our mule," or "I fell down the steps" were some of their replies.

Aunt Hattie was overtly emotional with sobbing fits, as she related this dark secret she had been keeping for years. The strange thing was, she said that she didn't know why she still had not revealed this cruelty in her childhood to anyone—even though her father and mother have long been dead, and she is now 90 years old. It could have something to do with the other big secret she had not revealed until now as her siblings were all told never to speak about it ever again.

One of my cousins admitted that his father used to severely spank him and his siblings, following the same pattern of abuse inflicted not only on him, but also his mother and siblings.

REFLECTION AND STATISTICS

The statistics are frightening. According to Bureau of Justice Statistics, Office of Justice Programs,

- 1 in 4 women will experience domestic violence.
- Women experience more than 4 million physical assaults and rapes because of their partners.
- Women are more likely to be killed by an intimate partner than men.
- Women ages 20 to 30 are at greatest risk of becoming victims of domestic violence.
- Every year, 1 in 3 women, who is a victim of homicide, is murdered by her current or former partner.

Domestic violence not only affects adults, but it affects children.

- Every year, more than 3 million children witness domestic violence in their homes.
- Children who live in homes where there is domestic violence also suffer abuse or neglect at higher rates.
- A 2005 Michigan study found children who witness domestic violence are more likely to have health problems.
- And a 2003 study found that children are more likely to inter-

vene when they witness severe violence against a parent, which can place a child at great risk for injury or even death.
- Statistics show that if victims or children of victims who witness such abuse may become perpetrators themselves when they get older and may carry that same violence into their marriage or relationships; that is, if they don't get counseling or some intervention.

You May Be Abused if...
- You are frightened by your partner's temper
- You are afraid to disagree with your partner
- You have been hit, kicked, or shoved by your partner
- You do not see friends or family because of your partner's jealousy
- You have been forced to have sex or have been afraid to say no to sex
- You have been forced to explain everything that you do, every place that you go, and every person that you see to avoid your partner's temper
- You believe that you cannot live without your partner or that you cannot get enough of your partner
- You believe that marriage will change your partner
- Your partner makes you feel worse about yourself
- You have fewer and fewer happy times together, and more and more of your time is spent on apologies, promises, anger, guilt, and fear

If you or a loved one or friend experiences any of these signs, seek help immediately (*There are resources listed in the Appendices section of this book that offer help for victims of domestic violence*).

THE OTHER BIG SECRET

Aunt Hattie was already red-eyed from sharing her story about the domestic violence that her mother and siblings had endured. She had to pause and catch her breath. She even asked me for water to ready herself to tell me the next big dark secret that she had been keeping inside since she was a child.

She shared through heaving tears and many pauses that her father took that same gun, that he had been threatening to shoot her mother and siblings and committed suicide by a self-inflicted gunshot wound to the head. His body fell on the floor with blood splattered everywhere. He managed to say while gasping for breath, "Now, y'all are free." He died soon afterward.

Aunt Hattie has wondered what her father really meant by those words and why he felt the need to kill himself for them to be free, instead of seeking help. She said that it seemed like days before the sheriff came to see the body and before the undertaker had it removed. She, her mother and siblings had to see their father's body lying on the floor in all that blood and with blood on the wall and other places now drying while waiting for the body to be removed. They were all devastated and traumatized witnessing such a travesty.

The funeral was held in Wilmington, North Carolina due to the family's disgrace and secret surrounding the suicide. Their grandmother, Janey Rosetta Henry, lived there. Aunt Hattie's brother, Lorenzo, was the only sibling their mother allowed to attend the funeral.

Aunt Hattie told me that the sheriff had the audacity to question her mother extensively as if her mother had something to do with her father's suicide. She shared that it was unbelievable that the authorities seemed to know about the domestic violence that her mother suffered yet had done nothing to help her and her children. Now, the sheriff had the mitigated gall to insinuate even that her mother may have had enough of the abuse and may have shot him.

After an investigation, her mother was cleared, but Social Services had become involved, had planned to take the children away from their mother and place them in foster homes. But apparently, her grandmother in Wilmington had some clout. Her grandmother had the siblings moved to Wilmington where she lived.

Aunt Sadie had already left home before the suicide and was living with their grandmother at the time in Wilmington. She refused to take the abuse any longer and knew she had to get out that hostile environment.

~

After the death of their father, their mother became ill and suffered from an unknown sickness with much excruciating pain in her body. Aunt Hattie thinks it may have been the result of years of physical blows and abuse that had taken a toll on her tired old body. She died a few years later and their brother, Lorenzo, became the patriarch of the family and took care of his siblings—all except Aunt Sadie. By this time, she had moved from Wilmington to Norfolk and was on her own.

Lorenzo rented a house in Wilmington with the help of his grandmother and Social Services. He cared for his remaining siblings until he met and married his wife, Jessie Mae. The other siblings visited Aunt Sadie in Norfolk several times and over a few summers. They met their spouses and eventually made Norfolk their home.

REFLECTION

Research shows that mental illness is common throughout the United States, affecting tens of millions of people each year. And what's most startling is that most people, who suffer from mental illness, don't get the help they desperately need.

Why would a person choose death over life? This question has been asked for centuries. Most of us regard suicide as an illicit, selfish act.

The Bible teaches us in 1 Corinthians 3:16–17, "Do you not know that you are God's temple and that God's Spirit dwells in you? If anyone destroys God's temple, God will destroy him. For God's temple is holy, and you are that temple." And Ecclesiastes 7:17, "Be not overly wicked, neither be a fool. Why should you die before your time?"

The National Institute of Mental Health indicates that 90 percent of all suicide "completers" display some form of diagnosable mental disorder. If that's the case, why do we have a suicide rate of 11 victims per 100,000 Americans? Almost the same figure it was fifty years ago. Nowadays, we have antidepressant drugs, crisis hotline centers, yet few people take advantage of these sources.

As a society, I suppose we've learned to accept there will always be those driven to take their own lives, However, the good news is, there are now plenty of resources available people can obtain to try and prevent suicide. This book offers hope, resources and assistance to someone you may know contemplating suicide.

HOW TO FIND HELP

For people who are not sure where to go seek help, talk to someone you trust—a doctor, nurse, social worker or religious leader or counselor. You can even go to a local university and ask for the departments of psychiatry or psychology. The Internet has a wealth of resources, as well. If the problem has escalated and there is a crisis, the local police or an emergency room doctor may be able to provide temporary help, until further help becomes available. The Crisis Hotline for Suicide Prevention is: 1-800-273-Talk or (1-800-273-8255).

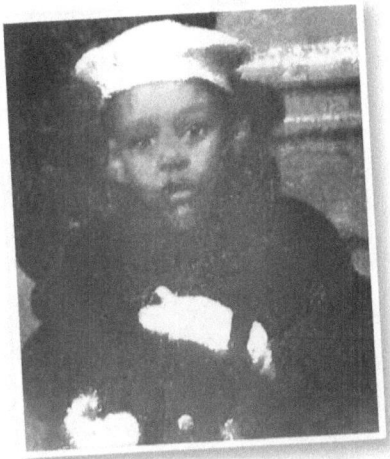

Hattie has an inquisitive look even at the tender age of five years old.

My loving stepmother Hilda "Teenie" Lee. I will always consider her my real mother.

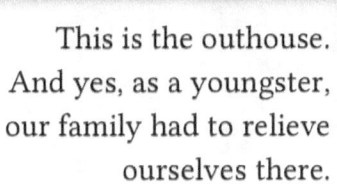

My Hero, My Father Samuel Neal, Jr.

This is the outhouse. And yes, as a youngster, our family had to relieve ourselves there.

Hattie as a teen, and as an adult at The two-room schoolhouse where her education began.

Hattie's Booker T. Washington High School Graduation picture.

Students of Farmville, VA R.R. Moton High School Protest its closing.

Hattie poses at a mosaic of civil rights hero Barbara Johns at the R. R. Moton Museum in Farmville, VA with Rev. J. Samuel Williams.

Hattie tours the campus of the R. R. Moton Museum.

"The Eyes Of The World Are On Us"—Written On The Wall Of The Simulated Tar & Tin Roof ("Chicken Coop") Structure.

My friends Reverend J. Samuel Williams and Joy Cabarrus Join me in the gallery of the R. R. Moton Museum in Farmville, VA.

My baby girl Cheryl below smiling about how beautiful she grew up to be!

Grandma's Girls

Charrell, Reagan & Cameron.

Charrell's new dress.

Hattie's granddaughters Reagan and Cameron Thomas are at a young age seasoned performers of dance, piano and acting.

Both girls are straight A students. Their hobbies include: Arts & Crafts, Drumming and Reading.

Thomas & Washington families enjoy Thanksgiving dinner.

My son Wayne and I enjoy some time in the kitchen.

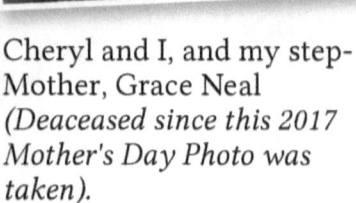

Cheryl and I, and my step-Mother, Grace Neal *(Deaceased since this 2017 Mother's Day Photo was taken).*

The Thomas family and I during Easter 2019.

Dr. Washington received a citation for the opening of her third boys home in Montgomery County, Maryland.

Aunt Hattie's Place | Truly Her Brother's Keeper

Over the years, Dr. Washington's annual AHP galas received tremendous support from the social and business communities.

From Retiring Professor To Aspiring Author

Dr. Washington is in demand for book signings, readings, speaking engagements and media appearances. Call 443-804-6545 for info.

Dr. Washington was selected "Featured Author" for her book at the 2016 & 2018 Congressional Black Caucus Convention (*shown here with the renowned Dr. Michael Eric Dyson and his award-winning book*).

~ PART TWO ~

Faith and Favor

CHAPTER 7

Aunt Hattie's Place:
My Brother's Keeper

"That's what 'My Brother's Keeper' is all about. Helping more of our young people stay on track. Providing the support that they need to think more broadly about their future. Building on what works— when it works, in those critical life-changing moments."

– PRESIDENT BARACK OBAMA, FEBRUARY 27, 2014

I've always believed in "creating" winners rather than just "picking" winners. In 1994 while serving as assistant superintendent of Baltimore Public Schools, in my regular interaction with students, I realized that many school children were foster children and did not have a safe, stable, and loving home, placing them at risk of becoming under-achievers and just another sad statistic.

As a result of my concern, I began to take foster children in my home while Social Services sought to place them in a permanent safe environment. I envisioned providing a home for many foster children, much like my own home and my childhood home in the country, where each child would receive the nurturing, love, guidance, and attention needed to develop to their fullest potential. I specifically wanted to help black males because they were more at risk of being placed in special education, dropping out of school, and eventually going to prison than other races.

In 1997, my vision became reality. I founded Aunt Hattie's Place, Incorporated, a non-profit organization that serves as residential facilities in the state of Maryland for male children in foster care who have been abused, abandoned, neglected, and have special educational needs. My organization provides a safe, stable, nurturing, and long-term home for them.

It took me three years to open Aunt Hattie's Place (AHP) and meet all the State and local regulations required to open the home. The irony of it all, I never planned on opening a group home for foster boys. That was not my intention. I just felt a need to rescue "youth with potential" who needed a good home-cooked meal and a warm bed in which to sleep at night. Normally, society calls these children "at risk." I prefer to use a positive approach when referring to these types of children. I call them "youth with potential."

~

Foster care is designed to be temporary placement for children when the parents cannot care for them. Nevertheless, I've discovered in twenty-plus-years of being a foster parent to many boys that they are in foster care long term and that they do well when they feel loved and part of a caring family unit. This feel of a family unit could very well be a group home setting if it's nurturing, stable and structured. I see my work at Aunt Hattie's Place as a "mission and a ministry", and my way of "giving back" and making a difference. Aunt Hattie's Place strives to erase the stigma associated with foster care by utilizing a family-oriented approach for children, which promotes a sense of belonging and accountability. This approach is a unique style that is engrained in the mission of Aunt

Hattie's Place. I look for that caring character trait to be present in the people I hire, as well.

Planning, developing, and acquiring the first home wasn't an easy task. It was uncharted territory to me. I had entered an undertaking that tested my faith and stamina, but eventually turned into a miracle, which I'll explain further in chapter ten. How many people will make that personal sacrifice? All of this goes back to my upbringing and who helped me along the way.

In 1997, I received a state license to open a group home. The year prior, I rented two townhomes next door to each other. At the time, it felt like a catch-22—I couldn't accept donations or raise money until I received approval as a 501(c)(3) entity, and I knew that the boys had to eat, and the rent had to be paid. Thus, until my application for 501(c)(3) designation was approved, I cashed in my annuity to help fund the first group home, making it operational by paying the rent, furnishing the townhomes, getting the electrical power turned on, and purchasing food and clothes for the boys. I now get reimbursed by the state of Maryland for each boy cared for, but it takes weeks for AHP to receive the reimbursement payments. I enlighten people all the time, who inquire about opening a group home, that your purpose can't be about making money. It must strictly be about helping and saving foster children, or you will quickly throw in the towel.

For those, who are considering building one, I do recommend partnering with organizations that will help you do the logistics. Back then, we had to do it all. You need lots of patience, persistence, and stamina. And, it starts with a plan. First, plan how the foster home will operate, including how you will obtain the capital. As I recall, it took two years to get my doctorate, but it took me $3^1/_2$ years to write the proposal for the group home and get it approved. I remember putting writing my memoir on hold because the group home proposal became all-consuming and the group home proposal became my book. I amassed enough paperwork to fill a four-inch binder, which consisted of the plan and the specific program requirements to satisfy all the Code of Maryland Regulations (COMAR) to open a group home.

While running and operating the first group home, I advanced in my career, eventually becoming the first female vice president of Coppin State University. I was overcome with gratitude after I discovered that I had gotten the position. To be honest, I didn't know if I could run the foster home and the university simultaneously. Both required my time, knowledge, and leadership abilities.

Many nights, I prayed to God for strength and He blessed me with it, along with wonderful staff, like my daughter Cheryl, who served as Executive Director of Aunt Hattie's Place; my stepsister Audrey Bailey, who is the Chair of my Board of Directors; and volunteers like my right arm, Julie Haskins-Turner, who was my executive assistant when I was vice president of Coppin State. I am also blessed to have generous people who donate money to help keep Aunt Hattie's Place running. I tell people all the time that we're in need of everything: cooks, housekeepers, typists. I need people who can run our database—the whole nine yards. Running a foster home is just like any other business, except it's a home.

On February 14, 1997, Aunt Hattie's Place officially opened its doors, providing a long-term home to eight foster boys, ages ranging from nine to thirteen years old. In January 1999, Aunt Hattie's Place was cited as a model group home by the Maryland State Department of Human Resources and Baltimore City Department of Social Services. In July 1999, after finding our ideal home, we relocated and expanded in West Baltimore City (Howard Park/Forest Park Community). The additional space allowed us to care for twelve more boys rather than the previous eight. In November 1999, we were awarded a grant from Baltimore City, under Mayor Kurt Schmoke, to assist with building renovations.

A year later, we were awarded a bond bill from the Maryland General Assembly to acquire, design, renovate and expand the house in West Baltimore. The bond bill was sponsored by the late Senator Clarence Blount and the late Delegate Howard "Pete" Rawlings with great support from Senator Lisa Gladden (then Delegate). In October 2001, the renovation and expansion were completed, and our

Ribbon Cutting Ceremony was held with over one hundred people showing their love and support.

THE STANDARDS OF AUNT HATTIE'S PLACE

Living at Aunt Hattie's Place is what I call a leadership training program. My staff and I are committed to equip young males with skills, education and discipline to become productive men in society. From the moment a young male walks through the door of Aunt Hattie's Place, I tell him, "My name is Dr. Hattie Washington; however, I like to be called Aunt Hattie, because we are family here at Aunt Hattie's Place."

I then set the rules. He is required to help with chores (i.e., mop the floors, clean the bathrooms, empty and recycle trash, do the laundry, and other household tasks). I required each young man to learn a musical instrument and a foreign language and play a sport, including either golf or tennis. I've read that learning to play a musical instrument helps young brains develop language skills. In addition, I wanted them to be culturally diverse, because when you are working with people and building relationships with them, it helps to have some perspective and understanding of their cultures.

To excel in school and in life, our young people, particularly young black males, need role models. If they don't have anyone to show them the right way or lead them down the right path, or even have a thriving person to emulate, they will make stupid mistakes that could affect them for the rest of their lives. Statistics show that our education system is failing young black males. Many are reading one to three years below grade level.

At Aunt Hattie's Place, we set standards for youth. We taught them skills that will benefit them throughout life. We enforced a strict dress code: No earrings; Pants must be up to your waist, not hanging down, showing your underwear; and, they were required to get a haircut every two weeks. Before leaving in the morning for school, they were to read the plaque that I had hanging on the wall by the door, which stated:

- I'm great.
- I'm smart.
- I have good manners.
- I'm lovable.
- I'm handsome. (They added handsome.)
- I'm thankful.

After residing in Aunt Hattie's Place, many of the young males, who came through our doors, have had fulfilling and successful lives. For over twenty years, Aunt Hattie's Place contributed to the community and society by being home to many young males. They have benefited from our programs and services. Many of our former residents have gone to become college students, attended graduate school, and after college, have become gainfully employed while living independently. There are quite a few of them who have pursued careers in the armed forces.

Society expected them to be lifelong failures. Their success is their validation that not all black males are thugs and prison bound. I am honored and at the same time humbled to say that my group home was cited by the Department of Human Resources as a model for other group homes, because of the significant progress many of my boys made in their academics, behavior, and self-esteem. This was because I, along with my administration, staff, the Board of Directors and our village of supporters, had high expectations of the young men and showed them love and stability.

~

Nothing prepared me for the challenges that we endured in opening the third home in Sandy Spring, Maryland. The five-car garage house was bequeathed to me by the late Robert Hill, a black homebuilder who was president and CEO of Sandy Spring

Construction Company in Maryland. Everyone called him Uncle Bob. He left the house to me two years before he died. His company built over two hundred houses in the area. He and his wife, the late Josephine Hill, had such generous hearts while living. Uncle Bob and Aunt Jo made contributions to different churches throughout the state of Maryland to help people who needed food and clothing. Uncle Bob even had his own gas pump on his property at the right end of the garage, where he would often allow friends to gas up their cars when they visited. His wife and I connected by way of our profession.

Sometime in the early 70s, they had a party at their house, and I was invited by another friend in Baltimore. When I saw Josephine Hill, I realized that I knew her from a teachers' meeting. We reconnected when I returned from overseas. I consider Josephine Hill the definition of a real lady, nurturing, serving others, and unselfish. I admired her so much. She was known to some as Jo, but I called her Aunt Jo and her husband, Uncle Bob. They were like my second parents and instantly became my mentors. I was moved by their kindness and generosity as I was not a biological niece, and they had relatives to whom they could have left the house.

Unbeknownst to me, they decided to leave the property to me some years earlier. Later, Uncle Bob told me that he and his wife were moved when I cashed in my annuity to help finance the first foster boys' group home in Baltimore's Eastside. They were touched by my commitment to this cause of helping foster children and decided then that they wanted to help.

THE HEART AND THE HEADS TO GET THE JOB DONE

I loved the synergy and the inspiration to do good that one feels when you go through a leadership class. I feel leadership classes are for leaders with the heart to make a difference. Leadership classes build self-confidence and wisdom and empower you to succeed.

You're in classes with like-minded people who also have the skills or the connections to get the job done. When I envisioned the third group home, I thought back and realized that every time I attended each of three previous leadership classes, the group was so motivational that I felt driven to open another group home.

This last boys' group home was no different; inspiration for it came from my Leadership Montgomery class. It took six years to build the third house. And all during the planning, development, and implementation stages, I thought: why is this taking so long? I thank God that I had special leadership groups that helped me along the journey. Kim Jones, Luana Dean, Ari Brooks, Muriel Ward, and others started the six-year process of opening the home on the five-car garage piece of property.

~

To begin the process of helping me with my vision of building this new "eco-friendly" foster boys group home in Sandy Spring, an outgoing and community-minded young man named Jeff Donohoe of my 2004 Leadership Montgomery Class, then dubbed by the entire group as "the best class," set up a meeting at my home and introduced me to other community-minded leaders who have become pivotal in making my vision a reality. Jeff, of Donohoe Construction Company, brought to the meeting attorney Emily J. Vaias of Linowes and Blocher LLP, who is an angel on earth, providing legal assistance, pro-bono, from 2004 to present; George T. Myers of GTM Architects; and Steve Tawes of Loiederman Soltesz Associates (now Soltesz).

All these God-sent individuals agreed to help initially pro bono, and they relentlessly and untiringly did everything from legal help with a Bond Bill, drawing up the architectural plans, and doing the engineering structural assessment to determine the feasibility of the vision as initial conceived. Shortly thereafter in the planning process, Jeff introduced us to Greg Dillon, founder of Dillon Development Partners, who also brought into the vision and joined the team as the project manager.

The new boys' group home was opened in May 2010 for eight young men after six years of persistence, lessons learned and divine intervention. By building this house, we realized a dream as well as a legacy. No expense was spared for this new handicapped-accessible house for foster boys with special needs; it included an elevator and numerous eco-friendly features, such as a tankless water system, energy-efficient appliances, and a non-toxic paint that would save money in the long run. Because physical exercise is crucial to growing children, especially boys considered hyperactive, the new group home has a swimming pool and a multi-purpose sports court, with a tennis and volleyball conversion. The basement has several pieces of donated exercise equipment, such as a treadmill, exercise bike, and weights.

The Board of Directors and a group of local supporters called the "Village Support Team" considered this group home a national model for the type of environment in which all foster children deserve to live. To us, this new home, as well as the group home in Baltimore City, has changed the concept of how a group home is supposed to look.

My foster sons were (and are) proud to bring friends home and gladly replied when their friends would ask, "Do you live here? I thought you lived in a group home?" To which, my foster sons boastfully and gleefully replied, "Yes, this is where I live, and this is a group home."

During the construction, I decided to give up the position of vice president of Coppin State University to dedicate more time to building the new home. I returned to the faculty as a full-time professor as I have always enjoyed teaching. It is a rewarding passion of mine to train teachers to teach and to reach all our students regardless of their present level of performance, their gender, diversity, family income, family makeup, and other differences.

Unfortunately, the State contract wasn't renewed for 2014 and beyond. A state initiative called "Place Matters," which places emphasis on finding permanent families for as many foster children as possible has sharply reduced the number of children in foster care. In an article written by Julie Bykowicz with the *Baltimore Sun* (October 2, 2009, p. 2) she wrote, "Under this new approach, the department focuses on reuniting foster children with their own families or keeping them in family settings, which has reduced the state's reliance on group home beds by nearly half."

I agree philosophically with this initiative and applaud the efforts for those children who have been properly placed and have thrived in their new environments. However, I am still concerned that follow-up data relative to the number of high school completions, college matriculations and/or success in job acquisition are not readily available on those children who were removed from group homes and resituated.

My point of reality is that I became a foster mother in my personal home first for several years before I opened a group home, but felt I needed more resources for the foster boys who had deep-seated issues that needed addressing in a more structured environment with sufficient staff to coordinate the services.

~

After many letters of support and an appeal, to no avail, we had no further recourse but to put this brand new "eco-friendly" group home up for sale in order to pay the bank the mortgage owed. Now facing homelessness, as I used my own personal home as collateral to partially fund this third foster home, my personal home had to be sold, along with the new foster home. Still, I continued to pray for a miracle. I kept a single candle lit in each window of my personal home as a symbol of hope and faith that someone would want to assist with this unfortunate dilemma and get involved with funding this worthy cause of saving foster children.

I once quoted in a newspaper article, "I would do it again in a heartbeat, because I believe the kids are worth it."

CHAPTER 8

"IF I Grow Up"

> *"Train up a child in the way he should go and when he is old, he will not depart from it."*
>
> **– PROVERBS 22:6 (NIV)**

"If I grow up." That line has struck a chord with me since the day I heard it. From a young age, we are encouraged to think of what job we want to do when we grow up. What contribution do we wish to make to the world? We're asked that question before we even learn how to tie our shoelaces. I had asked that question countless times at Aunt Hattie's Place, but on one summer evening, after eating a spaghetti dinner with my foster sons, I didn't get the answer of historically respectable professions—a doctor, a lawyer, an engineer—that I normally had gotten in the past. The response was, "If I grow up."

I looked at my foster son Lamont whose mother was on crack and whose father was murdered. Oh, my goodness. I couldn't believe what I just heard. To which I asked, curiously, "Did I hear you say, 'If you grow up›?"

He matter-of-factly replied, "Yes, because kids around my way don't git to grow up and be somebody."

"You don't think you'll grow up?" I asked, baffled.

He looked at me and began his story. His father was a high school dropout and sold drugs to support the family. And his mother had been on crack as far as he could remember. The reason he was placed in foster care was because his grandmother, the woman who had taken on the challenges of raising him, became senile and was placed in a nursing home. Lamont admitted to selling drugs and was hoping to get caught so that he could go to jail. There, he would get what he called "three hots and a cot."

I looked at him and asked, "What do three hots and a cot mean?"

Another one of my foster sons answered before Lamont could. "Aunt Hattie, it means three hot meals and a place to sleep in jail."

Now I was speechless. When my mind could finally process the things they were telling me, I said, "You mean you want to go to jail?" "Yes." They said, if it weren't for Aunt Hattie's Place, they would be homeless. In jail, at least they'd have a place to lay their head and something to eat.

One of my foster sons named Isaac added, "It's better than being homeless, shot by the police, or shot by drug dealers."

I became upset with them for thinking like that. I said, "If you go to jail, you'll get a record. Then you can't go to college because you can't get financial aid."

They told me that they felt the police were their enemy instead of Mr. Friendly. I was surprised to learn that many of them feel that they can't make a legitimate life. For some reason, they feel that the policemen are out to get them. I've heard many of my foster sons say, "Why try? I might as well live bad and steal a car, so I'll have a bed to sleep in and something to eat."

When these kids go to jail, I personally don't see social workers trying to change the system to keep them from entering the prison system.

~

Being positively influenced by my stepmother and elementary school teacher, Mrs. Brown, and after living what I call a slave-labor existence with Aunt Sadie, I prompted myself to articulate a purpose for my life. But, I'm one of the lucky ones. Many black kids feel defeated. Look at what has transpired in Ferguson. The police aren't looked at as Mr. Friendly, by our many black citizens, but as Mr. Enemy. Our black men have this "it's us against them" mentality.

It's difficult to disagree with them, or show them other instances to the contrary, when statistics proves otherwise and when one sees unarmed black teenagers being gunned down in the street by police and a black man like Eric Gardner, accused of selling loose cigarettes, suddenly held in a chokehold, telling the police, "I can't breathe," yet he is still choked, head pressed down into the concrete. But, by the same token, when black men react by cursing and disobeying police, the police will act with force.

I tell my foster sons all the time that you must look the part to be respected. The police officers are already scared and may react by using their weapons. We must educate our kids, or it will be the police who take a different approach when dealing with black youth.

Why does it take highly publicized tragedies for people to take a stand? We don't take a stand when it's black on black crime. In fact, I believe that we should take more of a stand. Economically, we must save all our children, especially the African-American male. They are the most feared, most hated most endangered and most targeted group than any other race or any other culture.

I personally believe that if any other race or culture had as many of their people in prison, on probation or parole, as there are in the African-American race, that it would be a crisis in that race or culture community.

~

In all my years of teaching and helping young African-American males, I've also learned that they are the most intelligent, witty, and inventive survivors, anytime they can maneuver the system the way they do to survive. Still, they are like a hamster on a wheel. Many are stuck, not able to get anywhere in life due to being mislabeled, undereducated, unloved, and having no available and consistent mentors.

The solution: give black males incentives to do well and stay on the right track. A community must put forth concerted efforts and aggressive programs, specifically for boys of color, to make them feel like they are part of the community. I believe there should be more non-threatening programs that provide a General Educational Development (GED), and as an incentive, the programs should offer a home-cooked meal while there. Let them know that getting an education is doable, possible and fun.

These programs should collaborate with high-schoolers, earning community service credit, and retirees to serve as mentors for anyone who pursues their GED or who is in high school and just needs that additional support. Obama's My Brother's Keeper and North Star initiatives, as well as former First Lady Michelle Obama's Reach Higher initiative, reinforce my belief of "Creating Winners," not just "Picking Winners."

When discussing what they wanted to be as a career option, my foster boys and my earlier classroom students would ask me, "How do I get to college? I don't have a clue." Although I can now respond with firsthand knowledge, which hadn't always been the case. A first-generation college student myself, when I attended Norfolk State, I didn't have a clue how to maneuver the application and admission process. Because of nice and friendly Norfolk State staff, I was assisted through the process. I've told my foster boys if they have the will to go to college; there will always be a way.

CREATING WINNERS, NOT PICKING WINNERS

Millions of people are stuck with criminal records for life, whether they knowingly committed a crime or did something immature and foolish. Having a criminal record can have a huge impact on a person getting a highly paying job, getting any federal or state aid or loans for school and difficulty in finding housing. People then give up and are stuck in the system. I think the biggest problem with our system is that we extend punishment beyond prison and jail time. I believe that we need programs to help erase certain minor criminal records of youth. If a youngster has cleaned himself or herself up and has proven themselves to at least three people who want to vouch for this person, those vouchers should be counted, and the person's record expunged.

If we had programs to erase criminal records of people, who made dumb choices or survival choices early in their youth, I think society would have fewer people in prison and more people holding down legitimate jobs and going to college. When decision makers espouse zero tolerance of infractions that will affect a person's entire future, I often think how many of these decision makers would have had a record or would have been in jail when they were young if they had been caught or if they had not been given another chance.

Lest we forget from whence we have come and how we got over, as the saying goes. The "creating winner" approach first starts with what I call, "The Three P's: **P**roactive, **P**revention, and **P**ositive." My approach has always been—whether in rearing my own daughters, teaching my special students or rearing my foster young men—being proactive in educating our children (provide students with upcoming school subject information prior to it being taught in school); preventing them from being another dropout statistic (anticipate what the students will need for success and integrate their strength and interests); and using positive strategies and approaches (make learning fun and give various realistic incentives) for them to learn.

These techniques worked for my daughters and my foster sons. Why not apply them in the classroom?

Another technique I used with my daughters, ever since they were in school, was called EASY-Learn (**E**arn **AS** **Y**ou Learn). My EASY-Learn technique involves rewarding children for their good grades in a consistent and systematic manner: Reward them $10 for every grade of "A," $5 for every "B," and if a "C" is made, the child owes the parent $20. Unless the grade of "C" is an improvement from an "F" or "D" grade; then they would earn $2. I opened a bank account for my daughters and encouraged them to save at least 60% of their earnings.

I am quite aware of the opinions of some who feel children should not be rewarded for making good grades or for doing well in school and that children should make good grades strictly for self-gratification alone. I beg to differ.

While philosophically, that sounds terrific, I haven't met any child or adult, for that matter, who didn't respond to positive incentives. Would most adults work for free, even if they enjoyed their job? Would they work for self-gratification without some reward for a job well done? I don't think so. I believe very few will.

At first, I thought my daughters may have earned good grades for the incentive, but later I observed that they earned good grades just for themselves. They developed greater self-esteem in the process. I use this same technique with my granddaughters, my cousins' children and my foster sons. Some of my foster sons' grades have gone from straight F's to C's, B's and even A's. I can see the great improvement in their grades every quarter to the extent that I tease them and say, "Whoa, Your grades are so fantastic this quarter that you are breaking the bank!" to which they will chuckle with a proud look on their face. I'll say compliments like, "Congratulations, I knew you were smart. I'm so proud of you . . . aren't you proud of yourself?" When they respond with the obvious, "Yes, ma'am," I would say, "Let me hear you say how proud you are of yourself," motivating them to continue to make good grades on their own.

Over the years, I've seen great improvement in youth, especially in black youth—many in my special education classrooms and at Aunt Hattie's Place. Working with them, I realize that most of them are misunderstood. Not all black youths are thugs and criminals as many are often stereotyped. I've discovered that they are ambitious and smart enough to start a business.

I recall one hot day on a busy corner where there was a red light, I saw four young black men, who looked to be in their early twenties, selling ice-cold bottled water. They had the timing of the red light–turning down to a science and sold water to several customers before the light turned green. I purchased a couple of bottles thinking, how enterprising. On other corners in Baltimore City, I saw black youth, called "Squeezie Kids," approaching cars at the red lights and squirting wiper fluid, and in some cases, just plain water, on the windshield of cars without permission and then wiping the windshields clean in a flash. Even if the drivers didn't wish to pay our boys, the drivers still received a friendly "Have a good day."

Even though these boys should have been in someone's classroom, if properly motivated and given the chance, they could do great things in life and would make wonderful employees or business owners. What a waste and such a shame for these youths to be so misunderstood and be prematurely written off as failures before they are even given a chance to succeed. They are smart enough to know what most of society thinks of them and smart enough to know that they must survive in this world, despite the low expectations of them and despite not being given an opportunity to put their brainpower into action.

Marian Wright Edelman outlines in her bestselling book *Ending the Cradle to Prison Pipeline and Mass Incarceration*, published by Common Dreams, that the crisis of mass incarceration of African-Americans has created an epidemic in the black community since slavery and negatively and financially affects not only blacks but also the entire country.

To be more profound and specific, Edelman indicates:

Black males have an imprisonment rate nearly seven times higher than white males and Hispanic males have an imprisonment rate over twice that of white males.

Mass incarceration is tearing fathers and mothers from children, and economically and politically disempowering millions by taking away the right to vote and ability to get a job and public benefits, in some states, after prison terms are served. One in nine black, one in 28 Hispanic and one in 57 white children have an incarcerated parent.

Mass incarceration has also become a powerful economic force and drain on taxpayers. Annual state spending on corrections tops $51 billion and states spend on average two and a half times more per prisoner than per public school pupil. I think this is a very dumb investment policy.

Federal spending on prisons totaled $6.6 billion in fiscal year 2012. An added danger driving mass incarceration is the privatization of prisons for profit. The Corrections Corporation of America, the largest private prison corporation, has proposed to 48 state governors that it will operate their prison systems for 20 years with a guaranteed 90 percent occupancy rate. A majority of all those incarcerated have committed nonviolent offenses.

Considering the recent cases, Michael Brown in Missouri, Eric Gardner in New York, Freddie Gray in Baltimore, and many other less publicized cases, several plans with recommendations have been developed by various groups and organizations that purport to be proactive, preventive, and positive. One such plan is by the National Urban League which outlines their 10-Point Plan for Police Reform and Accountability with the following Plan Recommendations:

- Widespread use of body cameras and dashboard cameras;
- Broken windows reform and implementation of twenty-first-century community policing model;

- Review and revision of police use of deadly force policies;
- Comprehensive retraining of all police;
- Comprehensive review and strengthening of police hiring standards;
- Appointment of special prosecutors to investigate police misconduct;
- Mandatory uniformed FBI reporting and audit of lethal force incidents involving all law enforcement;
- Creation and audit of national database of citizen complaints against police;
- Revision of National Police Accreditation System for mandatory use by law enforcement to be eligible for federal funds; and
- National comprehensive anti–racial profiling law.

A CRISIS

Our lives are not about us alone, but about others, especially about youth and how many we can save or influence. America is facing a crisis because the baby boomers (persons born from 1946 to 1964) are graying and have started to reach retirement age a few years ago. For the next thirteen years, most of them (us—I am in the first wave of baby boomers) will be retiring. This mass exodus will create a crisis and begs the answer to the vital question, "Who will replace the vast number of boomers and fill the positions that they will leave vacant?" Those include doctors, lawyers, engineers, teachers, social workers, nurses, and many other important positions. We have already begun to see shortages in many positions, such as the teaching field.

Many school systems have no recourse but to import foreign teachers from various countries to fill the positions, some who may have weak English-speaking skills; thus, making it difficult for many students to understand what is being taught. It's challenging enough for some students to learn and stay focused with a teacher whom they can understand and comprehend what's being taught, but this added challenge may be just the straw that creates a sense of pessimism in the students. They may internalize the lack of understanding personally and think they are stupid and can't learn; so why try, especially if the teacher conversely cannot understand the students—either their English or their collegial slang expressions common for that community.

Therefore, we need to save and educate ALL our youth. Parents, teachers, and mentors all play a vital role in a child's development, whether we do it because we believe the children deserve a chance or because we believe they have latent, untapped potential and want to help. The reality is that it's a must to make sure no student fails; the failure of students who are needed to replace retirees is not an option. Everyone must succeed.

Teaching differentiation strategies and community mentorship programs are needed to reach and follow students from cradle to the grave to ensure their success in school and life. If not, the results will become an economical crisis for the entire country, as well as a community threat. This crisis will affect the entire nation, and we will be a nation at risk.

The reason I opened Aunt Hattie's Place was to help foster males by providing these abused and abandoned boys with a chance to be all that they could be, especially the black male. I learned through my experiences as a public school teacher of special education children, with mostly black males in my classes, as I pointed out before, that all sorts of negative and low expectation statements were told to parents of these special students and foster children. Just a few of these such statements were: "Your child doesn't belong in my classroom because . . . *I'm not capable of educating your child . . . it takes a lot of time and energy to teach your child . . . your child is a troublemaker . . . your child has ADHD (Attention Deficit Hyperactivity Disorder) . . . your child should be placed on medication to behave right . . . your child is bipolar . . . it's a waste of time to teach your child because he's not going to be anything.*"

My stance is every child deserves an education. They deserve the right to be respected and loved. It troubles me when I see youth who do not belong in special education because they were mislabeled or misdiagnosed or even both.

I'll use a student I taught named John as an example. He was labeled by the school as a "bad kid." Teachers were on guard whenever they were in his presence. He seemingly had control over his classmates and the school. John did what he wanted and came to school when he felt like it. The class started at 7:30 AM, but John would walk in around ten and disrupt the class. He loved being the class clown or picking fights with other students. Ninety percent of the time, he looked angry and had an unhappy frown on his face.

Most of the students in my class were labeled misfits and were from the projects (public housing) and were left to fend for themselves. Because the school did not want to deal with him, he was passed to the next level regardless of his failing grades.

One day I had had enough of John's tardiness, his disruption and takeover of my class. I walked up to him and inquired about his lateness and admonished him for disrupting the class upon entering. He looked at me with the meanest set of eyes and replied, "F— you."

The words were so foreign to my ears that without realizing it, I had grabbed John by his shirt collar and held him against the wall. I spoke slowly and lowly so that he could understand that I meant business. Looking him in his eyes with a strange glare, as if I was possessed by the same demon he had in him, I said, "Don't you EVER use that language again in this classroom—show respect to your classmates and me. You are better than that. You got that?"

The look of shock on his face was utterly unforgettable. When I released him, he slowly slid down to the floor and started tearing up. Apparently, no one had every reprimanded him in a "tough-love" manner. I couldn't help myself. I started tearing up, too. It was something about this short pudgy-nose tough exterior kid that caused my heart to soften and feel empathy for his plight. I could see that deep down he was starving for love and attention, even if the attention were negative attention. He was crying for help, and it seemed like no one was listening.

Before I knew it I was stooping down to give John a hug and a soft pat on the back, saying no words, just a hug of compassion, a hug of consolation, a hug for time past of neglected hugs and a hug of forgiveness to let him know, let's start fresh. Although he used profanity at me, it was not really him talking to me. He was cursing at a society that had neglected him. He was a kid who was trying to survive in an environment that had written him off, where he couldn't do anything right.

All these feelings caused me to look in John's watery eyes and see his soul, which told me who he was and whose he was—a child of God.

When the other students saw my tears and me hugging John, several of them came over and asked was I okay. When I nodded "Yes," one of my students bent down and hugged me, and then he put his arm around John also. It wasn't long until another student came over and hugged me on another side with his other arm around John's shoulder. Other students followed suit and came over for a group hug. A moment later, I motioned the class back to their seats. I handed out tissues to everyone. They were crying, also. I don't know if they really understood why they were crying or why I was crying or even why John had tears in his eyes. But I do know that they felt the love in the classroom and wanted to be a part of it.

John was a changed student after that day. He and I had made a powerful connection. He came to school on time, began listening and obeying in class and eventually excelled in all his subjects. He became one of my top students. It was deeply satisfying to see John change from being the bully that everyone hated to a kind, striving and productive young gentleman. I have seen too many of these same type of students, over the years, who had been written off by the school, by the community or society as a "bad kid" or other such labels as "at-risk," "trouble maker," "retarded," "dysfunctional," and others as an excuse not to teach them or hold them accountable.

Subsequently, these students live up, or live down, to the expectation. They relegate themselves to a "self-fulfilling prophesy" mentality and make reality whatever is expected of them, be it negative or positive. What a waste of human potential which we cannot afford to keep let happening in our society—especially now being on the precipice of baby boomers mass retirement exodus of the job market.

My question for society is what makes some people so volatile? We tend to blame the offender, but conflict can result when a person feels a lack of love, has been mistreated or misunderstood, has not been given a chance or even a second chance. They feel hopeless and portray a "why even try" defeatist attitude.

Seeing so much of this "cliqueness" in the classroom over the years as a teacher, I made it a point to teach my daughters, when they were children, to make friends with those students who appear to be unpopular, who may not dress as nicely as other students and who are always alone. I would tell them to imagine how they would feel if no one talked to them.

There were many times when my daughters would come home excited. They would explain how they had made a new friend that day and the reactions of their popular friends and other classmates. My daughters could clearly see that because of their kindness that they made a less popular student happy just by their "Hello." They also shared that their popular friends followed their lead and showed friendship to this person as well. I told my daughters that it may have appeared to be a small thing to do, but it probably changed that person's entire life.

Footprints in the Sand

*One night I had a dream—
I dreamed I was walking along the beach with the Lord
and across the sky flashed scenes from my life.
For each scene I noticed two sets of footprints,
one belonged to me and the other to the Lord.
When the last scene of my life flashed before me,
I looked back at the footprints in the sand.
I noticed that many times along the path of my life,
there was only one set of footprints.
I also noticed that it happened at the very lowest
and saddest times in my life.
This really bothered me, and I questioned the Lord about it.
"Lord, you said that once I decided to follow you,
you would walk with me all the way,
but I have noticed that during the most troublesome times
in my life there is only one set of footprints.
I don›t understand why in times when I needed you most,
you should leave me."
The Lord replied, "My precious, precious child,
I love you and I would never, never leave you
during your times of trial and suffering.
«When you saw only one set of footprints,
it was then that I carried you."*

– MARY STEVENSON

CHAPTER 9

Mentor Mothers and Fathers

"Tell me and I forget, teach me and I may remember, involve me and I learn."

– BENJAMIN FRANKLIN

Definition of a Mentor: According to Merriam-Webster Dictionary, a Mentor is someone who teaches or gives help and advice to a less experienced and often younger person.

I truly believe that everyone has that special sixth sense and can instinctively feel a special connection to certain people they encounter along life's journey. These connections could have been intermittent, short-lived, or long-term, but I believe certain individuals are guardian angels, who enter our lives for a reason and a season. The longer I live, I don't believe that these people who we encounter in our life are a mistake or a coincidence; but that all of them are by design and are all a part of the big picture of our purpose for being here on this planet. Some people call it Karma; some call it serendipity; but I call it God's Favor in our lives.

I believe that if we would just stop and think retrospectively of all of those special people we have met, interacted with, who said or did something to enhance our spirit or encouraged us to keep moving forward in our lives, I am sure we can name many such guardian angels.

This chapter of my book on Mentor Mothers and Fathers would be much too long and would be the entire Memoir if I mentioned all of the persons I have encountered in my lifetime whom I feel were my many guardian angels who found favor with me and helped me along the way. However, due to space constraint, I will mention just a few of my most prominent mentor mothers and fathers. These people have dramatically touched my life and have influenced me. I will share briefly how they specifically made an indelible impact, but in no way am I able to do justice in words of their true impact to my mind, my heart, and the soul of the person I have become.

The interesting and most profound truism is that many of these mentors did not even know that they were being sought out and observed by me or that they were being emulated by me for some characteristic, trait, skill or mannerism that they possessed that I admired, respected and wished to acquire as part of my positive persona and well-being. With some of my mentors, it was an unspoken relationship or a feeling that they had found favor with me, and they had become my mentor; and I, their protégé—without anyone ever mentioning the word "mentor" or "mentee." Others would just take me under their wings and show me the ropes, so-to-say, in a new situation or a new job position.

I have found that most times, successful people consider it an honor and a sheer act of flattery when someone wants to be like them. Thusly, more people should try asking for mentorship early on and throughout their life. They will find more help than they can imagine.

I have listed some of my most laudable mentors in the chronological order of their encounter of my life, but in no means in any order of significance.

MENTOR MOTHERS

"MAMA" (HILDA "TEENIE" NEAL)

Mama, as I called her, was my adorable stepmother. I didn't discover that she wasn't my biological mother until I was twelve. To me, the title "stepmother" does not do justice to Mama, who was the most caring and loving mother that anyone could have. Her love in my early years was so profound and nurturing that it had a lasting impact on my life and on the type of person and mother that I have become.

Her unashamed expressions of her faith and her affection made everyone in her presence feel special. Though I felt that I was her favorite child, I later discovered in life that other siblings also felt that they were her favorite. This was such a profound revelation and such a remarkable gift to make everyone feel valued in our own unique way. This is yet another of her many nurturing traits that I try to emulate in life.

MRS. MAMIE DELL BROWN

Mrs. Brown was my first teacher in a two-room schoolhouse, Levi Elementary School, in Green Bay, Virginia from first to fourth grades (from 1953 to 1957). Mrs. Brown influenced me to become a teacher later in life.

She also was such a loving and nurturing teacher who utilized varied modes of teaching and learning to reach all her students. There were no students put in special education or written off as not being able to learn. In retrospect, she was practicing differentiation of instruction and "No Child Left Behind" before it was mandated by Congress some sixty years later. In other words, much of what I needed to know about teaching and learning and went to college to learn, I really learned in Mrs. Brown's country classroom in that two-room schoolhouse.

AUNT HATTIE (HATTIE KINDRED FENNER)

Aunt Hattie, my namesake after whom I was named, is the matriarch of my biological mother's side of the family as all her other siblings are deceased—Aunts Mattie and Arrie, Uncles Lorenzo and Roy. She soon will be 91-years-old. She still lives in her own home and has a wealth of family history, stories and experiences to share. I am enormously appreciative that she felt close enough to me when I interviewed her recently for this book to share the deep-seated and forbidden secrets which she had kept silent all these years.

I will be forever grateful to her for opening her home to keep my three siblings and me when the schools closed in Prince Edward County.

AUDREY BAILEY MEREDITH

Audrey is my older stepsister. Her mother was my dear stepmother, who was also named as one of my mentors. Audrey is my mentor, advisor, supporter, and role model. In addition to finding favor with her mother when I was growing up in Meherrin, I was also very close to Audrey, whose nickname was "Tootie Boo." She would comb my sisters' and my hair each day for school and would take the time to give me some compliment on whatever I was doing or had done or even what good manners I had. Knowing her as the giving and mature person that she was, she probably did the same for my other sisters. But I culled the belief that she would give me extra words of positive affirmations and encouragement.

She taught me many skills that I still remember today. She taught me how to properly iron a shirt and a blouse and how to make coleslaw from fresh shredded cabbage. She also would have me say the multiplication tables and the states of the USA and other pertinent information as she combed my hair. Audrey loved to dance, and I remember various dances she taught me such as the stroll and mash potato from American Bandstand. Upon retirement she joined the Board of Aunt Hattie's Place and has been the Board Chair for the last several years. She and many of her siblings attend the Zion Baptist Church in Baltimore where Pastor Marshal Prentice and the congregation have also been most supportive. Words cannot begin to express the wonder and the appreciation to her for exposing me to lifelong lessons, memories, and her mentorship.

HELEN H. CLARK ("AUNT HELEN")

Wife of the late Reverend Doctor Bishop Herman Clark ("Uncle Herman"). She encouraged me to serve in various positions in church. I found favor with her and Uncle Herman and was appointed over a period of rotation for all of us teenagers as Sunday School teacher, Church Announcer, choir member, usher, Sunday School Superintendent, and other events chair.

That mentorship of training us teenagers how to organize for community activities were life-long lessons. Her family took me in to stay with them when I was 6 months pregnant with my first daughter, Charrell, while my husband was overseas in the Navy. Aunt Helen was working on her master's degree in Teaching and taught me how to do research. She showed me first how to write a bibliography and put it on 5×7 index cards. Then, she taught me how to transfer the data from the index cards to the body of the thesis. She taught us how to type the thesis on a Corona typewriter (days before the computers for thesis writing).

These were lessons that I took into my acquisition of my master's degree and my subsequent doctorate—so did all her children: Dr. Vernon Clark, Dr. Herman Clark and Dr. Phyllis Clark.

DR. VELMA SPEIGHT-BUFORD

Dr. Speight was the Assistant State Superintendent of the Compensatory Division for the Maryland State Department of Education who hired me when I returned to the USA after living in Scotland and studying at Glasgow University. She found favor in me. I quickly considered her my mentor and role model. She was impressive as the only female Assistant State Superintendent (not to mention the only black female). She was smart, well dressed and a fantastic state leader.

I watched how this elegant lady interacted with all the Superintendents across the state and how she was so well respected—though outspoken. She had silk boxing gloves as she enforced the Federal Regulations for the Compensatory Division to ensure the Local Educational Agencies (LEAs) were implementing these laws compliant as a supplement, not a supplant.

She taught me how to be nail tough with the federal law enforcement, but also how to provide the superintendents with technical assistance, first and show them exactly what I was looking for from them as the leader and demonstrate to them how to evaluate their principals. Also, she taught me how to identify if the school spent the federal funds as a supplement—to the regular instructional budget as opposed as spending it on what was referred to as a supplant. She would send me to represent her at various meetings and conferences across the State to give remarks on her behalf, words of inspiration, and even a speech or two for her.

People would refer to me as "Dr. Velma Speight, Jr.," which was a great compliment to me. People would say that I acted and talked just like her. And, that I even dressed like her. She taught me how to dress professionally as a female executive—knee length suits, modest cut blouse, just enough makeup, no distraction of loud nail polish—and other professional demeanor. Dr. Speight was a classy fast-talking, energetic, enthusiastic person who believed in her cause and loved what she did. I admired how this black female executive could engender so much awe and respect from all the superintendents across the State, all of whom were white, except Baltimore City.

Her double major in mathematics and French from North Carolina Agricultural and Technical State University (A&T) gave her that intellectual abstract ability to analyze a situation and express herself every now and then with a French expression and overtone that I thought was quintessential. Her speaking French from time to time gave me the nod to speak more of my Greek from my living and teaching in Greece for over two years—though I have forgotten much of my Greek now from lack of use—as they say, "If you don't use it, you lose it."

After retiring from the MSDE, she moved back home to Greensboro, North Carolina and remained active by serving her alma mater, A & T University, as Director of the National Alumni Association and the first female chair of the Board of Trustees and served in other leadership roles. Dr. Speight-Buford, also known as "Miss Aggie Pride," was recently inducted into the National Black College Alumni Hall of Fame.

I chose her to be my mentor/role model because her leadership tutelage helped to prepare me for my next leadership roles as assistant superintendent of schools and vice president of a university. I had observed her organizational, management, and professional development skills and saw firsthand how she made hard decisions that were fair, effective and forward thinking. My leadership style, mannerism, and other leadership skills are a good replica of my pleasant memories of Dr. Speight's charisma, intellect, and style.

DR. GERALDINE WATERS

When I arrived at Coppin State University (CSU) on loan from the Baltimore City Public Schools (BCPS) for one year, I met Dr. Geraldine Waters. I was immediately impressed with her friendly smile and personality as well as her teaching style and her beautiful penmanship both on the chalkboard and on paper. Being assitant superintendent and going in and out of my many classrooms and getting a chance to see the lack of great penmanship on the board, since Mrs. Brown, her penmanship caught my eye. She was also a true professional with a wonderful and helpful collegiality spirit.

She seemed to be impressed with me and proud of me and made herself available to assist me every chance she got as a fellow faculty member. When I became the vice president, she overtly showed her pride as if I were her own kin. I also worked with one of her sisters, Shirley who was a hard worker and had much commitment to Coppin. Her other sister, Velma, who worked for the Department of Social Services, was instrumental in assisting me with my state license for a group home. Dr. Waters made herself available to support me in any number of activities and events, and I try to do the same for her and her family.

DR. DOROTHY IRENE HEIGHT
(March 24, 1912–April 20, 2010)

Dr. Height was the President for over 40 years of the National Council of Negro Women (NCNW) and now President Emeritus. I was honored and humbled to have received the Humanitarian Award for Community Service from the NCNW presented by her in 2009. Sitting next to Dorothy Height for that award program, I had extended time to really talk to this icon, but more importantly, I had time to listen to her wisdom and benefit from her advice. I shall always remember her words of encouragement and support as she indicated that she knew of my five-year challenge and obstacles I was facing then trying to build the new boys' home in Sandy Spring.

To that end, she challenged me and said, "Continue to have passion and compassion for your cause and then be persistent with your plan and your purpose. Never give up on causes that you feel passionate about." Those words were tremendously motivational to me and were just the "wind beneath my wings" I needed as we persisted another year to get the boys home finished and opened in 2010—after a six-year endeavor.

I felt extremely privileged to have been nominated for this Award by my NCNW section, the Potomac Valley Section (PVS) under the leadership then of President Ida Fletcher and through their Social Outreach Committee, chaired then by Jeanette Wolfe. They recognized the work of Aunt Hattie's Place with foster boys with special needs who are at risk of failing without interventions. The members of the NCNW–PVS have been staunch supporters of AHP, not only with donations but also with their time and talent through volunteerism and sponsorship of Thanksgiving Dinners, Summer Reading Program Kickoff Cookout, Christmas Presents and other support efforts.

While Queen Elizabeth is the amazing and well-dressed Queen of England (whom I admired and met when we lived in Scotland), Dr. Dorothy Height's well-coordinated outfits reminded me of our very own queen. To me, she was our United States queen who also carried herself in a most sophisticated and approachable royal manner. Being affected personally by the desegregation era, I was impressed to learn that she worked on Civil Rights issues with Dr. Martin Luther King and was with him on the podium when he delivered his "I Have a Dream" speech in 1963 (I was a junior in high school then). She was later recognized by Presidents Bush and Clinton, and was called the "the godmother of the Civil Right Movement and a hero to so many Americans" expressed in a statement by President Barack Obama at her death.

Lastly, I so admire one of Dr. Heights' quotes that says, "Greatness is not measured by what a man or woman accomplishes, but by the opposition he or she has overcome to reach his or her goals."

VICTORIA ROWELL

I selected Victoria as a mentor because I was (and am) impressed with her and grateful to her for giving of her time to be AHP's tenth Anniversary speaker pro bono. Being raised as a foster child herself, she could relate to our mission and program of raising 165 children and was receptive to come when I first met her.

We met at a reception sponsored by Freddie Mac in Washington, D.C., where she was guest speaker and did a book signing of her book *The Women Who Raised Me* (2007). When I asked her out of the blue whether she would come to speak for our tenth anniversary, she called her publicist over to get my information so she could check her schedule.

Frankly, I thought out of sight, out of mind and that I wouldn't hear anymore from her after that evening. To my surprise, I got a call a few days later from the publicist asking for the date and logistics. Fortunately for us, her schedule would allow her to come to Baltimore to be our speaker. That was fantastic that her schedule was free for our tenth anniversary date; however, I needed to know her fee in order to know if we should go any further. However, Ms. Rowell was currently on a national tour uplifting the profile of foster care as an advocate, which was sponsored by The Freddie Mac Foundation (FMF). This nationally high profiled foundation agreed to gift to AHP the costs of an honorarium, travel, lodging and meals for Ms. Rowell to be AHP's keynote speaker. I could not believe my ears.

Needless to say, the gala committee and I were stunned and felt highly favored that this popular American actress, dancer and advocate for foster children had consented to come and be with our Aunt

Hattie's Place tenth anniversary and that such a progressive and notable foundation such as The FMF would step in and provide us with the dollars to cover the costs. Victoria Rowell is well known for her role as Drucilla Winters on the daytime drama *The Young and the Restless* and her role as Dr. Amanda Bentley (medical examiner and pathologist) of the TV drama called *Diagnosis Murder*. There are any number of other films in which she had a role as an actress; however, her experience as a foster child and now her role as an author were paramount as she would share her heart-wrenching commitment, advocacy and inspiration for children growing up in the foster care system, as she did.

What was most striking when I picked her up from the airport on the day of the gala was her genuine interest in our program and what compelled me to open a home for foster children. She wanted to know more about AHP, about the selection of our boys and some of our challenges that we have faced in raising our young men over a long-term basis. She, in turn, shared a bit about her childhood in the foster care system and how she endured; and how my boys could do the same. I had read her book by the time I met her; therefore, I could understand how and why she could empathize with our cause of raising foster children.

Though exhausted, she stayed and took photos with each gala participant who wished to snap a photo of her or have one taken with her. Another act of sincere compassion was when her books didn't arrive until after the gala was over, she stayed up until way past 3:00 AM and personally autographed every book that the gala participants had purchased earlier that night. She left an indelible impression on me as well as on all who met her in that one night—which is why I felt compelled to name her as one of my mentors and wanted to showcase her on the cover of my first book. She has not forgotten from whence she came; but, more importantly, she created a foundation to do something to give back and pull other foster children through the system.

GRACE NEAL
(Has Since Passed at the Printing of this Revised Edition)

"Mom" (as my siblings and I called her) was our present stepmom who was married to my father when he passed in 1989. She has been very sweet and kind to all my father's children and took up much time with my two daughters as they were growing up. Whenever we would visit my father on holidays and special occasions, such as Father's Day and Birthdays, she always made us feel right at home and doted over the grandchildren.

Having just turned 90, she couldn't travel to visit us like she used to, but she kept up with all of us, including my daughters, Charrell and Cheryl. My daughters called her "Grandma" and Charrell sent her family photos each Christmas to keep her abreast of Cameron and Reagan (her great granddaughters) and how they were growing and progressing in school and their other activities.

Mom's favorite story she always repeated was the story of how my younger daughter, Cheryl, who, when she was about 4 years old, manipulated getting a piece of cake from her when knowing she was not allowed until after dinner. Subsequently, telling Cheryl that she was going to be a lawyer one day. In fact, Cheryl mentioned that story and motivational reason for becoming a lawyer when she wrote about this in her law school papers. Although Mom had children of her own (Charlene, Wesley, Saundra) when she married my father, she has treated all my father's children with much kindness, affectionate and attention. She was a faithful churchgoer and was loved by all. I must say, I have been truly blessed with the wives (stepmoms) that my father selected and who have been "mentor mothers" in my life.

EMILY VAIAS

I cannot say enough about this committed young lady who has been the pro bono attorney and "guardian angel" for AHP for over ten years now. Emily is not just an attorney, but she is also a partner with Linowes and Blocher Law Firm. You would never know it because she has been just as attentive, supportive and compassionate about the cause over the years. She has also consulted with any number of other attorneys in her firm as we encountered various other challenges and obstacles as we were building the new boys' home in Sandy Spring. She was introduced to me by my good friend and "brother" Jeff Donohoe, who was in my Leadership Montgomery (LM) 2004 class, and she was in another LM class as well.

She started out representing AHP through the Bond Bills process but has continued on assisting AHP in numerous other legal related matters—from meeting with another pro bono team (James T. Meyers of GTM Architects and Steve Tawes of Loiderman-Soltez Engineering Firm) that Jeff brought to the table; to vetting the construction contractors to assisting with the paperwork for acquiring a bank loan. After the house was completed and opened in 2010, she continued to represent AHP in any issues that involved follow up contractors and even donated personal funds and individual gifts for each of our foster boys.

When the State did not renew our contract, she prepared an appeal document on AHP's behalf and represented AHP at the Board of Appeals. Even now, with the Sandy Spring boys' home closed, she is still assisting AHP by communicating regularly with the bank's attorney, attending articulation meetings and preparing the proposal for AHP's Board of Directors to the bank. I consider Emily an extreme supporter par excellence to AHP of the cause but also a great friend.

No words here can fully give Emily and her entire committed law firm, who have no desire for recognition, all the credit due them that she and they richly deserve. I am so blessed to have found favor with them as I know they were put in my path for a reason—to help do God's work.

MENTOR FATHERS

THE LATE REVEREND DR. HERMAN CLARK
(Affectionately called "Uncle Herman")

Deceased now. Uncle Herman (and his wife, "Aunt Helen"—mentioned in Mentor Mothers earlier) was Pastor of the New Hope Church Of God In Christ (COGIC) in Norfolk and was my pastor from ninth grade (circa 1962) to years later—even after I traveled overseas and was back in the USA living in Maryland. He and his entire family became like family to me, and I felt comfortable enough to go stay with them when I was several months pregnant with my first child, Charrell, and my husband was in the navy and was going to be away overseas during the birth. He started pastoring in a small church of about twenty members—mostly family members—to a bigger church of about two hundred members to an even larger church that held roughly two thousand members.

He was not only an extraordinary preacher and eloquent speaker, but he was also a visionary of the future needs of his church congregants and the surrounding community. To that end, he did not hesitate to sacrifice his and Aunt Helen's own personal finances to expand the church and its breadth and depth in the community. Except for Bishop D. Lawrence Williams, Bishop Clark was one of the best preachers in the COGIC organizations. He had style, spoke properly (enunciated his words), acquired his degrees, and was a most intelligent and respected leader not only in the COGIC organization but also in the community at large. He and his wife, Aunt Helen, mentored me professionally and personally and pushed me to pursue whatever purpose God had for my life.

Like Bishop D. Lawrence Williams, his COGIC mentor and role model, Uncle Herman and Aunt Helen were also steadfast supporters of his members finishing high school and going further to some postsecondary program, community college or a four-year college. I suppose that support was an even more preeminent reason for me to cling to his family where all his children (Vernon, Herman and Phyllis) were expected to go to college. It was understood that the choice was not "if" they were going to college after graduating from high school, but rather "where"? And they all did.

He and Aunt Helen became the godparents of my first daughter, Charrell. After all, he did rush me to the hospital when I was staying with them and my water broke. His son, Dr. Vernon Clark (now deceased) and his wife, Ella (Rev./Dr. Ella Clark now) became the godparents of my other daughter, Cheryl. Uncle Herman also performed the marriage ceremony of Charrell, after completing her residency in medicine, to Sean Thomas (affectionately called, my "favorite" son-in-law). Uncle Herman was my spiritual mentor who talked the spiritual talk but also walked the Godly walk and lived the life as an example for all to follow.

BISHOP D. (DELANO) LAWRENCE WILLIAMS

Pastor of C. H. Mason Memorial Church Of God In Christ in Norfolk on Goff Street—which was considered the Mother Church of God in Christ (COGIC) founded by Bishop Charles Harrison Mason in 1906. After Bishop Mason's death in 1961, Bishop D. Lawrence Williams renamed the church in Bishop Mason's honor as a lasting memory and respect for his spiritual leadership and his life.

My first encounter with Bishop D. Lawrence Williams was as a teenager during one of the church's annual revivals which was the place to be for the black community. All other COGIC and other churches made their way to the Mother Church during this revival, called the convocation. Bishop Williams became a mentor and role model from the very first time I met him. He was such an intelligent, elegant, articulate, well dressed minister and community leader who was interested in motivating and challenging the youth as early as I can remember to pursue post-secondary education after graduating from high school. He had three sons (David, Joseph and Samuel) and a daughter (Jessie W. Boyette), and he and his wife had them to set the pace for us by going to various colleges themselves.

He took me under his wings and selected me for various roles in his church and even after I joined the New Hope Church COGIC where my pastor was Rev. Herman Clark. Bishop Williams still selected me to serve in several local and regional leadership roles, including participating in several regional conferences held in Roanoke, Virginia, and Memphis, Tennessee.

On one such occasion, I had the distinct pleasure to ride up to Roanoke with him and his lovely and equally elegant wife, who also was a person worth emulating—I loved her beautiful laced handkerchiefs and gloves she never left home without. That road trip was probably my first extended road trip out of town and to that part of the State. I felt honored and humbled to be asked to ride with our Bishop and First Lady to this regional conference, which included all the other churches in that regional district.

There were many lessons learned along the way about the inner workings of the church and where they saw me in the hierarchy in the future. They also were genuinely interested in me personally and my future endeavors. They even talked about the type of young man I need to seek for marriage and a family as I think they did for all young people in the church. However, I couldn't help but to think that they were hinting about one of their sons, in particular. I will leave it at that. My point here is that you never know who will find favor in you for whatever the reason and that favor can develop into life-long friendships that become "just like family," as they became.

THE LATE SOUTHALL BASS

The school photographer who had his organization, The Bachelor Benedict Social Club, to select and sponsor me for the Debutante Ball when I was in High School. I never knew why he found favor in me and decided to treat this country girl to a Cinderella experience.

It could have been that he noticed my sadness and loneliness (for back home) and felt sorry for me. I remember when I first met Mr. Bass in junior high at Jacox Junior High; he tried to get me to smile when he was taking our class photos. I didn't feel like smiling nor did I feel I had any reason to smile.

He had a calm and nurturing charisma about him and made it clear that he was not moving on until I smiled. When I did decide to give him a half smile, he remarked gleefully that I should smile more often because I had a lovely smile. I believed that he was genuine in his assessment of my smile and made me smile a bit more to which he snapped and snapped away. He became a mentor for me and made a point to stop by my homeroom to say hello whenever he was in school taking photos of various other classes.

But selecting me for the debutante Ball was just another gesture of his compassion and community service. The debutante committee, which consisted mostly of the wives of the club members, arranged for us to take charm lessons and ballroom dance lessons with our escort for the ball. I did feel like Cinderella at the Ball, except my loving stepmom back home was not the wicked stepmom in the Cinderella storybook. Rather, it was just the opposite.

My love for ballroom dancing could have also come from this experience for which I will always be grateful for the civic-mindedness and cultural enrichment exposure that Mr. Bass and his club provided this young home-sick girl from Meherrin.

THE LATE JOSEPHINE AND ROBERT ("AUNT JO" AND "UNCLE BOB") HILL

I had inherited a five-car garage house from renowned community leaders and philanthropists, Josephine and Robert ("Aunt Jo" and "Uncle Bob") Hill in Sandy Spring in Montgomery County, Maryland. Though no biological kin to me, I wondered why they (many persons respectfully called them "Aunt Jo" for Josephine and "Uncle

Bob") found favor in me to choose me to leave the property when there were biological relatives who deserved, and I am sure expected, to be left the property.

When asked, why me? He simply said that this was not a debate, that he was simply informing me of a decision that he and Aunt Jo had decided some years ago when they learned I had cashed in my annuity to help fund the first boys home in Baltimore while waiting six months to hear the results of my inspection for group home license. Nevertheless, I felt favored and compelled to do something of note with this special piece of property that would be a legacy to this couple who had done so much already in the community. In other words, I felt, "to whom much is given, much is required."

Uncle Bob was the founder and CEO of the Sandy Spring Construction Company and built, I am told, over 200 houses for persons and had financed a vast number of them. In fact, he had a photo book of many of the houses he built as well as accompanying small note pads of the payment arrangement for persons to pay for their newly built house. He told the story of his playing baseball and never missed a world series of Jackie Robinson, his good friend and baseball idol. He even has a photo of him as a pallbearer at Jackie Robinson's funeral.

The baseball field in Olney, Maryland, is named in Uncle Bob's honor and called the "Robert H. Hill Baseball Field"; it's where he threw out the first baseball for any number of baseball seasons. Because of his success in home building, he sported a Rolls Royce or his classic Excalibur car and was called upon often to use his cars for weddings, parades and other special occasions, which he graciously obliged.

Having his own gas pump in his yard by his five-car garage, he generously and often offered friends and relatives the opportunity to fill up their cars at his gas pump. Having been inducted into the Montgomery County Hall of Fame, he was well loved and respected in the community and was sought after for support by most politicians and other community leaders. Therefore, I am honored to have been selected by him and Aunt Jo to leave his home, which he built himself. I am even more touched and humbled to have been able to turn his home that he built into a national model to house and raise foster children, who had become wards of the State due to home life-styles and lack of structure that often led to neglect and abandonment.

I believe that his bequeathed home, which has been turned into a model boys' home, is an example of the ideal appearance of a group home for all foster children is indeed a legacy to him and Aunt Jo, of which I am sure he would be proud.

THE LATE DR. WALTER AMPREY

Dr. Amprey was the Superintendent of Baltimore City Public Schools from 1991 to 1997. I credit him for having confidence in me and hiring me in 1992 as one of his five new Assistant Superintendents to head up the Northwest Area which consisted of 30 schools and about 35,000 students. Dr. Amprey quickly became a stalwart leader and a mentor to me who had a positive and an aggressive agenda for the Baltimore City schools. He brought innovative initiatives to the school system and challenged us to know what federal legislation was on the horizon and to train our principals and teachers to begin implementing the laws even before they were authorized by the federal government.

One such law was the Special Education law (IDEA: Individuals with Disabilities Education Act) that called for including students with disabilities in the regular classroom. Another law was the Title 1/Chapter 1 law that called for supplemental funds to the school system be used on activities that included more critical thinking for those schools with high numbers or high percentages of low-income families. He believed in being proactive and preventive rather than being reactive.

Because he encouraged us to be creative in addressing the issues in our school districts, I was not surprised when he offered support to AHP when I started keeping the foster boys in our school system and was especially interested in the foster boys who were also in special education. I give him much credit for his support to me of several innovative programs in my northwest school district to increase attendance, reduce suspensions and improve academic performance. He also supported my becoming a foster parent to care for children in our system in need of a home and a good education.

His most salient impression on me was his thrust for the school system of a concept that he called "Efficacy" which purports that "Smart is not what you are; smart is what you can get." He believed that if students believed in themselves and were willing to work hard, they could achieve and get to be smart. As a result, they would become smart and develop higher esteem in the process.

Dr. Amprey was ahead of his times and went on to form his own educational consulting company, Amprey & Associates, and shared his leadership skills nationwide. He still found time to provide mentorship and advice to me in my role as VP of Coppin and even served on a committee as we planned for the Coppin's centennial. As well, he visited the boys' home in Baltimore and shared his personal experience with the young men and offered his support through his network of stakeholders, encouragement and donations.

DR. GEORGE TAYLOR AND SOE FAMILY

I give Dr. George Taylor credit for my coming to Coppin in the first place. I was placed at Coppin on loan supposedly for one year from Baltimore City when I was Special Assistant to the Superintendent in charge of Special Education compliance. I wrote a federal grant to the Office of Special Education Programs with Dr. Taylor who was then Chair of the Special Education Department in the Education Division (now called the School of Education, SOE). Since Baltimore City was in a consent decree at that time for not adequately serving special education students, my new job was to develop a plan to show due diligence that Baltimore City was demonstrating progress to meet the needs of the special education students.

Since there was a shortage of special education teachers, our grant was to select regular teachers and retrain them as special education teachers in a master's degree program. The grant was to train a cohort of 20 regular teachers a year for five years (totaling 100 teachers); however, the selected trained teachers had to commit to teaching special education students in their regular classroom for at least five years in exchange for the carrot of acquiring a master's degree free of charge. Dr. Taylor and I worked hand in hand with getting this grant written and approved and implemented.

Therefore, after the grant was funded, he convinced me and the superintendent, Dr. Amprey, that the grant would be expeditiously implemented if I were on campus where I could also teach some of the initial core courses. During my tenure at Coppin, Dr. Taylor has been a true mentor as he also became my boss when I joined the faculty in the special education department. He is a great writer and has written numerous textbooks and other educational chapters in other books. As we served on various committees, presented workshops and trained teachers together over the years, he always expressed appreciation for my work and encouraged me to continue to be creative.

Dr. Taylor has retired now after 44 dedicated years at Coppin and is enjoying another chapter in his life. He leaves big shoes to fill in our Teaching and Learning Department and at Coppin in general.

A "special tribute" was given him at the well-attended Retirement Brunch and written on this Retirement Program that said: "Dr. Taylor, we wish you Godspeed & Bon Voyage as you embark upon another 'chapter' of your life. You have enriched our lives, just knowing and working with you, and the lives of all of those you have touched over the 44 years you have served Coppin and the community. Much Respect, Admiration and Appreciation, From Your friends and colleagues of the Special Education Department, Teaching & Learning Department, the Entire School of Education & The Coppin Family."

DR. CALVIN BURNETT
(Former President of Coppin State University)

Dr. Burnett made an unprecedented decision to appoint me as the first female Vice President of Coppin. This out-of-the-box decision was noteworthy for his confidence in my skills and ability to raise money for this historic and unsung hero college. Not only did I respect his intellect and leadership style, I was also impressed with his unwavering commitment to this college and worked tirelessly to keep it a thriving institution—even when there were subtle intentions of merging the college with other institutions.

He always demonstrated unwavering support to me for all of the innovative techniques and creative ideas to raise funds: such as the first annual galas, inaugural golf tournament, monthly grant newsletter of available grants, the amount and deadline; hosting a weekly cable TV show (called Coppin Pride); purchasing the first internet radio license; establishing a grant-writing lab and assisting each department with grant opportunities; coordinating a high percentage of participation in the United Way campaign; selecting many new Foundation Board members who knew how to raise funds; and others.

Retiring after 32 years dedicated to Coppin, he still watched over Coppin and other institutions as he was appointed for one term as Secretary of MHEC (Maryland Higher Education Commission). He and his wife, Greta (Dr. Greta Burnett) have remained close friends, mentors and supportive of all my endeavors at Coppin as well as Aunt Hattie's Place.

REVEREND DR. HAYWOOD A. ROBINSON III AND THE TPCBC FAMILY

Pastor Robinson, his wife, First Lady Renee, and the entire congregation of The People's Community Baptist Church (TPCBC) have served as mentors, family, friends and supporters. Since Dennis Williams and John Macklin from my Leadership Montgomery 2004 Class were members of TPCBC, I visited one Sunday and decided later to join. Pastor Robinson was not the pastor of TPCBC then for he was the pastor of Calvary Baptist in Baltimore. Calvary was only a few blocks away from my foster boys' home in Baltimore and the members were very involved and supportive to that boys' home.

My daughter Cheryl attended that church, and I would drive up to Baltimore from Sandy Spring many Sundays to hear Pastor Robinson preach (and sing and play the piano). I was in awe of his God-given gifts. And his wife, First Lady Renee, was also so loving and participated with the women's auxiliary that came to cook for the boys.

But that trek took my entire Sunday, and I had decided to join a church closer to home. I was not aware at the time that this same pastor whom I would travel miles to hear on Sunday was even in the running to be the pastor of the very same church I had decided to join in Montgomery county, The People's Community Baptist Church (TPCBC). It had to be divine intervention as he and the entire new TPCBC congregation embraced the idea of building a new boys' home in Sandy Spring to care for additional foster boys. At each step of the way, especially at the setbacks and the denials, he and the TPCBC family continued to pray and offered words of encouragement and inspiration as well as church and individual donations. Pastor Robinson would tell me that a delay is not necessarily a denial or that things will happen when they are supposed to happen and to keep the faith.

Through the entire six years to build the boys home and after opening, he and the church family have done everything from writing letters of support, attended hearings, volunteered, tutored, cooked, sponsored various activities, field trips and trainings for the boys, and many other supportive ways. Pastor Robinson also co-chaired (with Rev. Dr. Henry Davis, Pastor of First Baptist Church of Highland Park) a support group called C-FBI (Coalition of Faith-Based Institutions) of about thirty inter-faith institutions for a call-to-action purpose of assisting AHP in raising the foster boys through their time (mentorship), talent (tutoring and other training) and/or treasures (regular and consistent donations).

The C-FBI met quarterly and rotated the meeting between the Baltimore boys' home to the Sandy Spring home. They had guest speakers of pastors from various faith institutions: Just to name a few, Rev. Kecia Ford of Sharp Street United Methodist Church; Rev. Kenneth Nelson of Seneca Community Church; Rev. T. Kenneth Venable and First Lady Gene, of Clinton AME Zion Church; Min. La Verne Wilson of Charis Worship Center Ministries; Rev. Lisa Holloway of Circle Fellowship at Riderwood Center in Silver Spring; Mrs. Bettie Hoover of the Friends Meeting; Rev. Donald Kelly of Olive Branch Community Church; Rev. Marshal Prentice of Zion Baptist Church in Baltimore; college president, Dr. Mortimer Neufville of Coppin; and others.

The TPCBC family has remained vigilant and steadfast in their support of the one Baltimore boys' home since the Sandy Spring boys' home closed as a result of the State's initiative to reduce group home foster care. Pastor Robinson and my TPCBC family have kept the faith with me and have continued to pray that God's Will will be done, and His purpose and His plan will be revealed. I consider my entire church family as mentors and "guardian angels" for whom I feel especially blessed and highly favored.

DENNIS K. WILLIAMS

I met Dennis in my Leadership Montgomery class of 2004 and he quickly became my good friend and adopted brother. I became close friends also with his mother (Emma) before she passed and his sister, Juanita. He also introduced me to Delegate Herman Taylor, who sponsored a Bond Bill in Annapolis for the partial funding to construct the new boys' home in Sandy Spring.

Dennis died from cancer a few years later (2009) but left many lifelong influences in the church and the community. Juanita is carrying on his and Emma's legacy of commitment to AHP by serving now on AHP Board of Directors and chairing the Public Relations Committee.

OTHER MENTORS AND ROLE MODELS

DELEGATE HERMAN L. TAYLOR
And the District 14 Delegation

I first met Delegate Herman Taylor in 2004 through a fellow Leadership Montgomery class member (Dennis Williams, mentioned above) who introduced him to my program/rescue mission of caring for foster children in Maryland and my vision to build another boys' home in Sandy Spring. I was impressed that it did not take him long to understand our mission and became passionate about our population of children—as he was passionate about other similar causes that cared for the less fortunate and vulnerable citizens of our County and State.

At the time, he was a two-term Delegate to the House of Delegates representing District 14 along with then Senator Rona Kramer and Delegates Karen Montgomery (now Senator Montgomery) and Anne Kaiser.

During the ten years since I have known Herman, I have watched him perform his community servant duties selflessly and untiringly as he championed many worthy causes. I have never met anyone who cares more about his community and his State than Herman Taylor. His boundless energy and devotion show in the countless ways as he "pays it forward" in any endeavor he passionately pursues.

He boldly took on my project of opening a home for foster boys that, at the time was not popular with a few community folks who would rather help "these type of children" from afar, but just NIMBY ("Not In My Back Yard"). He and a local village support team and my team of Leadership Montgomery graduates met with many civic and community groups to share the vision and the plans. He also sponsored a bond bill to obtain partial funds to construct this third foster boys' home in Sandy Spring and collaborated with our other District 14 representatives who joined him to support the bill and other related follow-up letter writing.

Subsequently, Herman assisted in a wide array of other support tasks from mentoring the young men, arranging trips, sending other business and like-minded persons to see the program and meet our young men, to being present for our annual galas and giving words of encouragement on various programs. The other District 14 Delegates and other Montgomery and State legislators came on board and supported the fine young men in the program.

Though no longer a Delegate, Herman still shows his great continuous commitment in many other ways as he serves the community in a more global and systemic manner working with minority and other businesses—being a minority business owner himself. Everyone who meets and knows Herman will agree that these are just a few of his many attributes to describe him: Respected, genuine, dedicated, committed, knowledgeable, passionate, caring, fair, trustworthy, and driven. You can understand why I consider him to be a mentor brother and a great role model for our young men to emulate.

LEADERSHIP CLASSES

I need to give tremendous credit and accolades to each one of the leadership classes I underwent in my various career leadership roles since settling in Maryland after returning from living in Scotland for several years. I could be considered the "Leadership Junkie" or the "Leadership Queen" as I took four Leadership classes starting in 1994 and the last in 2004. Before I share briefly about each class, I would first like to say that each of the Leadership Programs was superb and was incredibly informative and crucial to whatever my new leadership role happened to be. I highly recommend that all persons, who are new to various leadership roles, take a leadership class in the county and/or State where your stakeholders are.

Not only did I meet a wide array of other leaders in the State in various roles, but I also got to hear different perspectives on issues from governmental, business and non-profit participants. Also, the classes traveled to various parts of the city or county and the state to meet the stakeholders and to see firsthand the programs and agencies that make them run smoothly. I met and maintained numerous lasting friendships and long-term supporters who found favor in my mission and helped my dream of making a difference to become a reality.

A. GBC (Greater Baltimore Committee) in 1994

My very first leadership class was the GBC in 1994 when I was Assistant Superintendent of Baltimore City Public Schools, and the GBC was under the leadership of Jon Houbolt, the Executive Director. This class was an eye opener to the many issues and needs of the city and challenged all of us to think of existing programs or create one that could make a difference. That challenge piqued my sensitivity and my desire to do something more permanent with more wrap-around services for the foster boys whom I was presently keeping in my personal home as a foster mom.

With the encouragement and support of Jon and my class ("the Best class"), I mustered the courage to begin the arduous three-year ordeal of satisfying the regulations to make this dream a reality—that is, to open a group home for foster boys, despite the fact that statistics indicated that foster boys are the greatest at-risk population. Jon and my classmates encouraged me on step by step even when the class was over. Several members have been constant and long-term support sister/brother mentors, such as Marsha Jews, Dr. Weldon ("Gary") Fleming, Dana Peterson, and others.

B. Leadership Maryland in 1997

My next leadership class was Leadership Maryland taken in 1997 under the leadership of Nancy Wolfe (now Nancy Minieri, who has recently retired). This class was taken when I was a new Vice President of Coppin State in charge of fundraising, and this Leadership class gave me more of a statewide perspective of the issues and problems as well as the agencies and possible solutions that could contribute to the successes of various collaborative programs. Again, this class ("The Best Class") was a varied mixture of classmates from the business, government, non-profit and civic community which made for stimulating conversations, discussions and problem-solving ideas and action-oriented processes.

Utilizing the collaborative skills and networking of my staunch 1997 leadership classmates, I was able to complete, that very same year, all the State and local regulations and officially opened Aunt Hattie's Place, Inc., a non-profit residential facility (a group home) for foster boys. My Leadership classmates got on board and supported the opening in February 1997, and most of them have been personally and/or financially involved on a long-term basis.

I must mention the generosity of John "Denny" Murray (deceased now) who found favor in our program and purchased a new 15-seat passenger van for the boys' home. Some three years later he surprised us with two brand new SUVs. Wide-eyed, mouth open wide and speechless with tears galore, I remember Denny saying, "Good, you can't speak; because I don't want any thank-yous anyway." After a tearful silent hug, he simply looked at me and said, "I am glad that I can help. Just keep on doing what you are doing." He was an amazing and generous person who continued his support until he passed.

Many other classmates also helped in their own way with either their time, their talent and/or their treasures, such as Kathryn Turner, Scott Wilfong, Dr. Marie Washington, Guttrie Smith, Dr. Charlene Nunley, Wayne Clarke and others. I love my Leadership classmates and Nancy, the Executive Director, who also would network and have other students from other classes to get in touch if she felt we could enhance each other's program or collaborate on certain resources.

C. Leadership Baltimore County in 2002

My next Leadership class was with Leadership Baltimore County in 2002 under the leadership of Eileen Hettleman, the Executive Director and Founder. This leadership class was taken after AHP had received a Bond Bill to be able to move from the east side of Baltimore to a larger house on the west side. As well, AHP was expanding to another location in Randallstown in Baltimore County, and I felt I wanted to know the county better and the players and stakeholders for the best coordinated services for the boys' home there. It was a no brainer at this point because of the rich experiences I had already enjoyed with the other two leadership program; therefore, I took the Leadership Baltimore County program.

As I expected, the experience was beneficial and comprehensive and allowed me to get to know the County and programs therein as never before—even though I lived in the County for over 15 years and sent my daughters to the middle and high schools there. Just riding around with the fire department and the police was an awesome experience and gave me a better appreciation for the work these persons do to keep our citizens safe. This class ("The best class") also became involved with the boys' home and performed many volunteer hands-on activities with the boys, and they also participated in our annual gala and other mentorship opportunities.

D. Leadership Montgomery County in 2004

The last leadership "so far" was the Leadership Montgomery County in 2004 under the leadership of Esther Newman (I affectionately refer to as "Ma Esther"), the Executive Director and Founder. This magnificent class ("The 'Bestest' class") was directly involved from the beginning and is responsible for the newly built foster boys home built in Sandy Spring in Montgomery County. After sharing my desire and vision to my class, I was encouraged once again by them as well as Esther and Kati (the program director and Esther's right-hand extraordinaire) to make that vision a reality. The whole class rallied behind me and coaxed me to move forward.

There was a cadre of persons from the class who took an extra interest in the boys' home project and were by my side, and who have been there long term and unconditionally. I cannot say enough about Jeff Donohue, Barbara Henry, Nancy Becker, John Macklin, Georgette "Gigi" Godwin, Melody K. Eaton, Jon Rosen and Dennis Williams (deceased now). Other significant supporters are Muriel Ward, Ari Brooks, Luana Dean, Kim Jones, George Simms, Henry Lee, Sara Watkins, Mary Kane, Christine Sorge, Ed Fone and many other classmates who have been supportive in any way, including my good and dear friend, Eliot Pfanstiehl, the facilitator.

E. Worth Mentioning: ELIOT PFANSTIEHL

The Leadership Facilitator for all my leadership programs, except the Baltimore County Leadership. When my daughter, Cheryl, went through two leadership classes, GBC in 2000 and Leadership Maryland in 2003, Eliot was also her facilitator whom she highly regards. He is an icon in his own right and continuously had new and fresh ideas, approaches and issues to present to the classes in an exceptional and creative manner.

He has been a tireless supporter to AHP in numerous ways, from writing letters of support to the county and the State, offering to testify before the county and/or State as well as hosting the boys at several performances at The Strathmore Music Center in Bethesda, Maryland where he is CEO and Founder of Strathmore Foundation, Inc.

PRESIDENT BILL CLINTON

I met President Clinton several time during his presidency at different events when I was VP of Coppin. One such event was at a NAFEO (National Association for Equal Opportunity in Higher Education) Annual Banquet as I sat at a reserved table close to the dais where President Clinton spoke. After his speech I was afforded the opportunity to meet the president and say hello. The President was very friendly and approachable and even took a minute and asked me which university I represented. To which I answered, "Coppin State College in Baltimore, Maryland," as I moved on for others in line to say hello (at this time, Coppin was still a college, not a university.)

Then, I met him again a year or so later at an annual banquet for the White House Initiative for HBCUs (Historically Black Colleges and Universities). Again, a way was made for me to say hello to President Clinton. To my surprise, he seemed to remember me and gave me a warm reception and asked again what university I represented. To which I again answered, "Coppin State College in . . . " To my surprise, before I could finish the rest of my sentence, he replied, "Ay Yes, Baltimore." I was dumbstruck at his recall and merely nodded my head. I had heard that Clinton had a tremendous memory of faces, facts and figures, but I was at a loss for words and incredibly impressed that he seemed to remember my cherished college—which is really a hidden oasis amid inner-city Baltimore. I smiled approvingly as I moved on as other persons were waiting to say hello.

Of course, I didn't delude myself that the president really remembered me from Adam (or should I say, from Eve). He was just being the utmost politician or, at best, was being gracious and now knew that Coppin State was in Baltimore. Whatever the reason for his memory, I respected his resourcefulness along with his charming persona which made each person feel that he was talking directly to him or her at that moment. I felt that way myself and noticed that same charisma as he spoke to everyone—which is a gift that a very few people possess.

Then, as fate and favor would have it, several months later he ended up on Coppin's campus campaigning for Kathleen Kennedy Townsend when she was running for governor. She was then Lieutenant Governor for Governor Glendening and was nominated by the Democrats to run for governor of Maryland. I don't know exactly how and why he and his entourage ended up selecting Coppin's campus for the campaign, but since my office was responsible for public relations, I was directly involved with the planning, greeting and orchestrating the campaign's press conference. He even spent a few minutes in my PR office as he took a short break before the press conference.

Therefore, my photographer snapped several photos of President Clinton and me as we chatted before and after the press conference and during his time on campus (see photo on front cover of book).

I found that same charisma as he graciously took time and met everyone who wanted to shake his hand. I consider President Clinton one of my Mentor Fathers (more like my mentor brother—as he is a baby boomer like I am). I admire the impact of his many social programs that he initiated as president and influenced in educational programs, particularly his support to HBCUs. Also, I can easily understand why he was considered by many African Americans as "The first Black President." He just seemed so comfortable and genuinely at ease around Blacks and other people of color.

After all, Vernon Jordan, one of his most respected confidants and best friend, was affably referred to as "The First Friend." I would love to have president Clinton to visit the new eco-friendly boys home we built in Sandy Spring that is closed now and/or the boys' home still open in Baltimore City—which is about three miles from Coppin—to meet our outstanding young men who are struggling to take advantage of their second (and some third) chance being at AHP.

MICHELLE OBAMA

Although First Lady Michelle Obama is only a few years older than my daughters, she is indeed an icon and a role model for me, and for them, to emulate. Having a daughter who is an attorney as she is, I have an affinity for her and the terrific job she is doing as the First Lady. I am especially fascinated by her various initiatives concerning and affecting children and young adults. For example, some of her noted and impressive programs are as follows:

A. "Let's Move" Initiative
The purpose of this program is to address the epidemic of childhood obesity that plagues a large percentage of our children. As a former teacher, I support her initiative to bring more physical activity back to the school and the community. As a busy working mom, I could also relate to the need for this initiative that put emphasis on helping busy moms and other care providers how to do healthy eating and cooking. She demonstrates with her own family how to prepare fresh, nutritious and affordable meals.

B. "Reach Higher" Campaign
The purpose of this initiative closely aligns with AHP's goal and that of Coppin State and other similar programs which encourages students to take their studies past secondary school and attend a four-year college, community college or a professional training program. Her Reach Higher initiative supports and is aligned with President Obama's North Star Initiative where he pledges to have America with the highest proportion of college graduates in the world by 2020. One initiative is akin to the other one. A student must first graduate from high school Reach Higher before entering a post-secondary program. For more information, see the Appendix of this book or visit http://obamawhitehouse.archives.gov/reach-higher

C. The Near Peer Mentoring College Challenge

The Near Peer Mentoring College Challenge initiative is interesting and innovative, and it combines mentorship of college student groups and officials with high school incoming students and community service. This initiative promotes having these college students to reach back and help other students, especially first-generation college students and students from underserved communities, to facilitate the quagmire of paperwork to get enrolled and obtain financial aid.

For more detailed information of this initiative and the most recent happenings, see the Appendix of this book or visit: http://www.whitehouse.gov/reach-higher/near-peer-commencement.

PRESIDENT BARACK OBAMA

I am honored to name my President, Barack Obama, as one of my Mentors—who has no way of knowing that he is my mentor and that he gives me encouragement and inspiration to continue making a difference through community service and giving back. With my mother dying at the early age of 28 and my thinking I would not live much longer beyond her age, I still must pinch myself to realize that I have lived long enough to see a Black President and Black First Lady in the "White" House. It makes me so proud that I could burst with personal fulfillment, as if they were my very own son and daughter and granddaughters.

Fulfillment also because of the trials, challenges and sacrifices my family and I had to endure and overcome in order to achieve and succeed despite the desegregation era in Prince Edward County. And, now to witness not only his re-election, but also the re-election of such a fine man as our president, who is also intelligent, spiritual, a negotiator, collaborator, sensitive, health conscious, cool calm and collected, and brave and decisive lead me to believe that he, too, is highly favored. He is a loving and affectionate husband who respects an intelligent wife, a doting father of two adorable and well-mannered daughters (I can relate as I, too, have two daughters and two granddaughters—who are about Malia's and Sasha's age). He is always a dapper dresser (except for those Mom's blue jeans he wore one day and was teased in a fun way). He is a role model for people of color, particularly black males, as well as a role model in many ways for anyone and everyone to emulate.

Further, I am enormously impressed by his stamina, optimism and his drive to make a difference in spite of the negativism and obstacles that he has had to endure since being in office as the president. His calm demeanor, intellect, and gentlemanly style have earned him unspoken respect, I believe, from even his staunchest adversaries.

I am sure he is keenly aware that institutional racism is alive and well and though no one has the gall to come right out and say so, but much of the supposedly definitive opposition and objection to his policies, ideas, procedures, appointments, etc. are due to generational and inbred racism. The objections, I believe, have little to do with whether his ideas are salient or that they will help the masses, and simply object because they can and more pronounced is because of a deep-seated resentment that this Black man and his lovely family are living in and enjoying all of the accouterments of the highest office in our US of A. That is, The POTUS (President of The United States).

When President Obama said during his last State of the Union Speech, "I have no more campaigns to run . . . I know because I won both of them," I sensed that he was getting geared up to make a mark on any number of the initiatives that he had promised the American people that he would implement—with or without the cooperation of his opponents.

Several of President Obama's pivotal initiatives that I especially respect, support and think are akin to what we are trying to do with my foster boys' homes, Aunt Hattie's Place, are as follows: My Brother's Keeper Initiative, The North Star Initiative, and Free Community College for everyone and others.

A. My Brother's Keeper Initiative

President Obama realized the concern for the chronic gap for boys and young men of color and expressed it thusly in his Memorandum of Understanding:

". . . persistent gaps remain in employment, educational outcomes, and career skills for many boys and young men of color throughout their lifetime.

Many boys and young men of color will arrive at kindergarten less prepared than their peers in early language and literacy skills, leaving them less likely to finish school. Labor-force participation rates for young men of color have dropped, and far too many lack the skills they need to succeed. The disproportionate number of African American and Hispanic young men who are unemployed or involved in the criminal justice system undermines family and community stability and is a drag on State and Federal budgets.

And, young men of color are far more likely to be victims of murder than their white peers, accounting for almost half of the country's murder victims each year. These outcomes are troubling, and they represent only a portion of the social and economic cost to our Nation when the full potential of so many boys and young men is left unrealized.

By focusing on the critical challenges, risk factors, and opportunities for boys and young men of color at key life stages, we can improve their long-term outcomes and ability to contribute to the Nation's competiveness, economic mobility and growth, and a civil society. Unlocking their full potential will benefit not only them, but all Americans.

Therefore, I am establishing the My Brother's Keeper initiative, an interagency effort to improve measurably the expected educational and life outcomes and address the persistent opportunity gaps faced by boys and young men of color. The initiative will help us determine the public and private efforts that are working and how to expand upon them, how the Federal Government"s own policies and programs can better support these efforts, and how to better involve State and local officials, the private sector, and the philanthropic community.

By the authority vested in me as President by the Constitution and the laws of the United States of America, I hereby direct the following:

Section 1. **My Brother's Keeper Task Force.** (a) There is established a My Brother's Keeper Task Force (Task Force) to develop a coordinated Federal effort to improve significantly the expected life outcomes for boys and young men of color (including **African Americans, Hispanic Americans, and Native Americans**).

Source: https://obamawhitehouse.archives.gov/my-brothers-keeper

B. The North Star Initiative
Another ambitious initiative I admire that President Obama implemented was his North Star 2020 Initiative. Being a baby boomer, I feel that this new initiative is planning ahead not only for the graying of the baby boomers who will be retiring in masses during the next decade, but he is also endeavoring to return America to the lead position of college graduates of teachers, doctors, lawyers, engineers and other such positions by 2020. I agree with this aggressive new initiative of the President, as well does First Lady Michelle, as they (and I) can relate to the difficulties of acquiring a college education without assistance. Therefore, I support this North Star initiative. Michelle said it succinctly when she said, "There is nothing more important to this nation's future than investing in our young people, and education is at the top of the priority list."

C. Free Community College
Having lived in Scotland for several years where college education is free if students make the score to be admitted, I see President Obama's plan for free community college, that he outlined in his State of the Union Speech, is moving in that same direction. Modeled on the State of Tennessee where they offer two years of guaranteed free community college, president Obama's plan would pay tuition for students maintaining a GPA of 2.5 or higher and making plans to transfer to a four-year college.

IN SUMMARY OF THIS MENTOR MOTHERS AND FATHERS CHAPTER

My only regret is that I didn't seek out more of my mentors and share with them how they influenced and impacted my life before their death. That's on my "Bucket List" now; that is, to share with as many of the persons whom I used as role models and whom I respected for whatever reason. I endeavor to let them know that they mattered while they yet live. In other words, give them their "flowers while they can still smell the fragrance."

CHAPTER 10

Miracles:
Divine Intervention

The Webster's definition of a miracle is, ***"an unusual or wonderful event that is Believed to be caused by the power of God."***
There have been many inexplicable miracles that have happened to me and caused me to think often of one of my favorite poems, "The Footprints in the Sand" where God was carrying me when I only saw one set of footprints. I have discovered in life that many times when you're going through a crisis that you don't have time to think about how you're going to get through it. You just muster up the strength and the will to just keep moving forward. When something unpleasant happens in our life, we've got to keep the faith.

Blessed are those who believe in a divine entity as compared to those who know the answer up front and, therefore, don't have to believe blindly and rely on faith to pull them through tough situations.

As I encounter life's challenges and support family and friends who are going through their own life's challenges, I recall a sermon my pastor preached one Sunday that was so impactful that I think of it daily. In essence, he indicated that being intelligent human beings, we sometimes have a disconnection between our cognitive faith and our affective faith—meaning, if we can't reason in our mind about what has happened and know exactly how or why it has happened, we question why we should believe in God, when all of the signs point to certain defeat. Then my pastor explained that faith is based on a feeling and a belief that God will work it all out for those who trust and love the Lord. Sometimes, we, humans, can be too smart for our own good leaving nothing to chance if we can't figure it out logically or as some people say, "If the numbers don't add up."

One writer explained, faith is a belief akin to the wind. You believe that it exists, although you can't see it. You see signs of wind's existence through its effect on our surroundings and it tickles your skin.

THE HOUSE: IN YOUR DREAMS

There are some who say they believe, but don't demonstrate their faith during a test. But we should remember that the teacher is always quiet during a test, so we should simply believe and not be fearful. Usually, when I think of trials, the story of Job in the Bible comes to mind. Job was a devout and righteous man to whom God allowed tragedies to happen to test his faith. He lost his wealth, his property, good name, health, including his children. He suffered through many trials, but divine interventions brought miracles that he wasn't expecting. While there have been numerous divine interventions in my life, and I don't have room in this memoir to mention them all, I am compelled to highlight a few of the most prominent ones.

I recall the moment that one of my foster sons was hit by a car while playing in the middle of the street on the east side of Baltimore. I was devastated because his leg was broken as a result of the accident. A few weeks after the accident, I experienced a strong sense of urgency while meeting with a realtor and preparing to sign the paperwork on another two-story house. You see, the year before, I had purchased two townhomes that were next door to each other to house my foster children. The townhomes had a tiny front yard and an alley in the back. They were just too small, and the neighborhood was just too dangerous. The boys needed a place where there was an open space to play that was not littered with contaminated needles and broken liquor bottles. But, as I was about to close on the house, something just did not feel right about this house. I was hesitant, even though the realtor was pushing very hard to close the deal. I looked at my daughter, Cheryl, who was there to support me and then I looked in the realtor's eyes and said, "No. I cannot sign these papers because this is not my house. I don't get the right feeling for this house," to which the realtor asked in a disappointing tone, "What is it that you are trying to feel?"

I could see the disappointment on his face as I tried to explain what I meant but couldn't. Nevertheless, my mind was made up, and I bided him a good day.

But something strange and wonderful happened. My daughter Cheryl was with me. I continued driving then something caused me to look up. And there it was. The house of my dreams! I immediately slammed on my brakes. I stopped the car in the middle of the one-way street. I said to my daughter, "That's my house."

I had stopped so abruptly that I didn't even notice a car behind me until I got an angry honk from the driver, which brought me out of my trance. I quickly pulled over to the side of the street and said with an assured grin, "That is my next boys group home. I know it. I can feel it." I said so confidently that Cheryl said, "Ma, how can that be? That house is not for sale. It doesn't have a For Sale sign." I responded with wide eyes, "I don't know how, but I am sure that's going to be our next boys' home. I know it."

As I took a closer look at the house, I realized it was the same house that I had seen in my recurring dreams. I thought this house was particularly lovely, a red-brick Victorian with a round stately dormer. It felt quite eerie knowing that the very house I had dreamt of existed. I immediately felt a need to inquire about purchasing this house. I quickly picked up my car phone and dialed my board member who was in real estate and inquired about the house. My board member indicated that he knew the house well and that the woman, who resided there, was not interested in selling her house. He told me to forget about it.

"But this is my next boys' home," I responded. "I need to meet her and explain to her that I've seen this house in my dreams." Still, all I kept hearing from my realtor was that I was wasting my time.

I approached the house regardless and knocked at the door. In seconds, I heard a gruff voice asking, "Who is it?"

~

The youth who ended up in my care were often preteens, who had bounced from one place to the next. I wanted them to have a spacious house with a big backyard. And the townhouses were just too small, and the neighborhood was just too dangerous.

I gave her my name and soon she appeared at the door with an equally crossed look on her face as if I had disturbed her from her watching her soap operas. No sooner than I opened my mouth, she blurted, "My house is not up for sale and you need to leave."

I was immediately caught off guard, but I had to go inside this house. I had to see for myself if this was the same house that I had dreamt about. I looked at her and said, "I don't know how to explain this to you, but this is going to be my next house."

The woman, who looked to be in her early seventies said, "I keep telling you that this house is not for sale. Do you see a For Sale sign?"

I turned to look at the yard. There wasn't one, as my daughter had already pointed out earlier. I looked back at her undaunted and told her my story of raising foster boys. "They are not 'problem kids,'" I said. "They are 'kids with problems' and just need a second chance. And some of them a third chance."

"Are you a teacher?" she asked, to which I replied, "Yes." She stared at me for a moment then told me that she, too, was a teacher but retired now. We connected, and it wasn't long until she invited me inside her house. She formally introduced herself as Mrs. Smith. She told me that she had taught for over thirty years in Baltimore City schools. Hearing about my mission of raising abused and neglected foster boys, she revealed that her greatest love and reward of teaching was being able to reach her "knuckle-headed" black boys, as she tough-lovingly described them. I could feel that she was softening as she offered to give me a brief tour of her house.

As she showed me around the house, I knew where every nook, cranny and corner was located, to the point where she shouted at her son, "Bob, you've had women in my house?"

He replied, "No, Ma, I've never seen this lady before in my life. I don't even know her."

I looked at her and validated his statement and said that I had never seen him before either. I told her that I had been having recurring dreams about this unique house for my foster boys, but I never knew that such a house existed. And, what was even more baffling, was that I knew where everything was in that house and how the present rooms were arranged. It still puzzles me today. The only explanation is that it was God's divine intervention at work.

After Mrs. Smith and I shared stories about teaching and laughed in retrospect, although things weren't always so funny at the time, later that day, I returned to her house with all eight of my boys in tow. My foster boys wooed her unintentionally. They first gave her a big hug and then huddled together on the living room floor at her feet and sang gospel songs and recited portions of Dr. Martin Luther

King's "I Have a Dream" speech to her to which she wiped tears from her eyes, and so did I.

Not surprisingly because of divine interventions, Mrs. Smith reconsidered and decided to sell her home to Aunt Hattie's Place, which would become the boys' new home with a large fenced in backyard. As it turned out, Mrs. Smith shared that she had wanted to eventually move back to her hometown of Tennessee and wanted her home to be used for something special. She didn't know quite what that was but was waiting for the "right nudge" as she put it. Therefore, feeling good that her home would be put to good use, she could now plan to move back home with a good conscience.

A few days later at one of my board meetings, I explained the divine intervention regarding the house. One of my members who was in real estate informed me many people had tried to buy Mrs. Smith's beautiful and distinctive house over the years—even himself, but she wasn't selling. The board member looked at me with unbelievable eyes and said, "I'm never going to doubt you again."

After Mrs. Smith consented to sell her house, I soon realized that we didn't have sufficient funds to purchase it. I prayed to God for a miracle. And, the Lord did just that. Weeks later, Cheryl and I were invited to an important breakfast. This was on a Saturday morning when I felt like lying in bed. I'll never forget. It was raining and cloudy that day. I found myself getting up and getting dressed as if I were out of body and could not control my actions. As I was leaving home and getting into my car headed to the breakfast, I saw a rainbow in the clouds. "Oh, how beautiful!" I thought, staring at it for a moment as the rain had stopped, and a warm feeling came over me like a gentle wind.

THE BOND BILL: YOU NEED A BB

At the breakfast, I was seated beside a nice young lady named Lisa Gladden, who was a Delegate for the House of Representatives of the

State of Maryland at the time. Delegate Gladden, my daughter, and I instantly connected and immediately struck up a conversation. While munching on fruit and bagels, I told her my story of trying to purchase a house for foster boys and not having enough money. *"You need a bond bill,"* she quickly told me. I didn't know the first thing about a bond bill nor how to go about getting one. I felt like a fish out of water. But I was soon relieved when I learned not only did Delegate Gladden know the proper procedure to obtain a bond bill, but she also formally introduced me to a senator and a delegate seated at other tables who could help get me one.

Senator Clarence Blount and Delegate Howard "Pete" Rawlings, both very influential men, happened to be seated next to each other. After Delegate Gladden had told them what I needed, they both said almost simultaneously, "We'll sponsor it."

God had intervened again and was on our side that cold rainy morning and revealed the whole reason I was supposed to be at that breakfast in the first place.

THE COMPLAINT: NIMBY (Not In My Backyard)

Things didn't run quite as smoothly as I thought. There were some challenges. After Delegate Gladden put the paperwork in motion for the bond bill and word got out that a boys group home was coming to the neighborhood, a man, who lived across the street from Mrs. Smith's house, protested because he didn't want "these types of kids" living in his neighborhood. He fought our efforts as best he could. He went to court and filed a complaint. My team had 90 days to respond to his protest, which we did immediately. He had 90 days to counter our appeal and he waited until about the eightieth day to do so. We had to go back to court and listen to his reason for protesting. Not only did he explain to the court his reasons for not wanting the group home in his neighborhood, but also, he told the local newspapers, and the media. To prove how divine intervention manifested itself, the disgruntled man thought he was holding us up and stalling the process, when actually he was giving us time to wait for the bond bill to be approved and giving Mrs. Smith time to pack up her household, especially since she had been living there for almost thirty years.

After about an eight-month ordeal, his case was thrown out on his third court complaint. A week later, our bond bill passed. Subsequently, my contractor gutted the entire house and added another 5000 square feet on the back for a larger kitchen and arranged the interior just as I had dreamed the boys' home would be on the inside. I also built a deck on the back and a wraparound porch on the front.

THE DOCTORATE DILEMMA: FINISH NOW OR LATER

Another divine intervention was the time I was completing my doctorate degree in 1987 from the University of Maryland College Park. I had an inexplicable and compelling urge to finish my doctorate that December rather than the following May as was my initial plan. However, I found myself staying up every night that fall for three weeks in a row, writing and studying while maintaining a full-time job. I'd go to work that morning, and then it was off to class that evening. During those days, my life was devoted to my daughters, my husband, and my schoolwork. I had a heavy load of responsibility, but I was determined to push through the rough terrain.

Having cooked dinner, washed a load of clothes and checked my daughters' homework, I would kiss my family goodnight and journey downstairs to the basement and work on my dissertation. There, I would read, research and write all night, then when morning came, I would cook breakfast for the family, shower, get dressed and head off to my typist to drop off what I had written that previous night. This grueling routine continued for weeks that fall until I finally completed my doctorate. God gave me the strength and the tenacity to finish in December 1987. My family, including my cousin and his wife from Virginia Beach and friends were all so proud of my accomplishment—becoming the first doctor of education in the family. While I was also pleased with this extraordinary accomplishment, I think I was even more thankful and relieved that this torturous anguish was finally over.

Then, lo and behold, as my elders would say, my dear beloved father unexpectedly had a stroke in March of that following year and became incapacitated. He needed around-the-clock care which vacillated between the hospital, home, the hospital again and the nursing home. Although I had sisters and a brother and several step and half siblings to assist with his care, he named me as his power of attorney. I therefore became responsible for his primary care and was dedicated to his well-being for that period.

My routine schedule was leaving home in Baltimore County about 5:00 AM to go to his house in East Baltimore, before heading to work. I made sure the live-in health care provider was taking care of him. At the time, I was working downtown Baltimore at the Maryland State Department of Education. Leaving work and coming back to his house and staying until about 11:00 PM and then hiking back to Baltimore County for a few hours of sleep, after chores at home, was my daily routine. I continued this exhausting schedule until my father died peacefully two years later. My family and I had him buried in the veterans' cemetery in Baltimore.

I followed my father's advice, "Never give up no matter how high the mountain." He was a man who taught me many lessons because he loved me unconditionally, and I love him. I miss him dearly. I followed his instructions of getting a good education; therefore, I excelled in both high school and college, and graduate school was no exception. His high expectation prompted me to earn a BS Degree in Elementary Education from Norfolk State University with a concentration in Special Education, a Master's Degree in Counseling Psychology from Ball State University, while teaching in beautiful Athens, Greece in an overseas program, and then a doctorate from

University of Maryland, College Park in Curriculum and Instruction.

My father lived to see me complete my doctorate. It became crystal clear why God gave me that compelling urge and burst of energy to complete my doctorate that December rather than that following May. Though there were other siblings, my father appointed me as his power of attorney, and I became responsible for his total care and provided and coordinated all the health services from home, hospital, and eventually the nursing home for the next two years until his death.

Some people may call it a coincidence that I finished in December and my father had a stroke that following March, but I call it divine intervention. I strongly believe that God knew that I would not have finished my doctorate after my father's stroke, because for the next two years, my father became my #1 priority. And, I believe that God knew I would not have gone back to finish after my father's death.

CHAPTER 11

Lessons Learned

"When pride comes, then comes disgrace,
but with humility comes wisdom."

– PROVERBS 11:2 (NIV)

As I think of my dear father, a man who sacrificed much, so that my siblings and I could have a better life than he had, I get emotional. My father knew my temperament and my way of reacting in situations, so for him to make the sacrifice to send my brother, my two sisters, and me to Norfolk to live with our biological mother's sisters, so that we could continue to receive adequate education, I think hurt him more than it hurt us. But he knew education would be the key to our success in life. I didn't see it then, but I see it now. There is a saying that I like and use quite a bit: **Vision without**

Action is just a Dream; Action without Vision is just wasting time; but Vision with Action can change the World.

Therefore, let's go forth and do Dream, but also put your Dream and your vision into an action plan to make a difference in our world. However, in all our planning, remember this verse: "A man's heart plans his course; but the Lord directs his steps." Proverbs 16:9 (KJV).

ESCAPED THE FIRE

A few weeks before the publication of this memoir, I experienced a major fire in my home that I've lived for over 13 years. Although devastated, I'm grateful that the Lord touched me and woke me up that morning. I was able to escape a burning house with injuries that have since healed. Presently, I'm in temporary lodging until I can find a permanent home, but I'm not upset in the least. Thinking back, after the Lord woke me up, I naively went to investigate the source of the smoke and called 911, who told me to get out of the house immediately. I quickly put on a pair of jeans over my pajamas, grabbed a shawl, my cell phone, purse and laptop and rushed out through the garage. By that time, there was smoke everywhere.

I started feeling sick right after leaving the house and arriving at my neighbors across the street where I was rushed to the hospital and treated for smoke inhalation and carbon monoxide poisoning. While I am proud of myself for having a working smoke detector with batteries, I am thankful that God is the one who woke me up. It was a miracle that I even heard the detector, as exhausted as I was when I went to bed. I had been burning the midnight oil writing my book. I very well could have been overcome with the smoke and carbon monoxide and not even heard the alarm. With the vast amount of damage that was done to my house, it is a miracle I escaped with my life. Material things become secondary and put in their proper place, when all you have is the clothes on your back and don't have a place to sleep. Basically, I became homeless in a flash—which can happen to any of us in the blink of an eye. That's why it is paramount that we know who we are and whose we are.

~

The lessons learned in this tragic incident are:

Know WHO We Are
"For what does a man profited, if he shall gain the whole world, and lose his own soul?" according to Matthew 16:26 (KJV). We should know who we are—apart from all our stuff, all our trappings we own and identify our importance and our status by what we own. Then, if your belongings are taken away by whatever means—man-made or natural disaster, we should not lose our sense of identity but continue to have faith that God will take care of us. After all, He made the universe and owns all the riches and dwellings within and at His Will can share them with us or help us to be happy and feel blessed with less stuff but more love of the beauty of His nature.

Another lesson out of the ashes of the fire is, "For we brought nothing into the world, and it is certain we can carry nothing out." According to Timothy 6:7 (NIV). In other words, we cannot take any material things with us when we leave this world. Therefore, we need to stop hoarding stuff and calculating our self-worth and happiness by the amount of stuff we possess. Although I like nice things and have worked hard to acquire many of the things I want in life, I felt a strong sense of gratitude for being favored to just be alive by escaping the fire.

When I left my burning house with almost nothing and had to virtually start all over with acquiring items, it gave me a greater appreciation for each day. Now, I seemed to gaze the world through different lenses and started noticing more of the little things in nature and in family and special friends—especially those who called and helped, left messages, texts and even those who were persistence and wanted to just hear my voice.

At the hospital I was told that I was lucky to have awakened with the vast amount of carbon monoxide in my lungs. But I told them that my God is not ordinary. He is an awesome God who works miracles. And that, I was not lucky to be alive. Rather, I am blessed to be alive. He favored me, yet again and woke me up to continue to do His work.

~

Over the years, I've learned from lessons that have encouraged me to keep moving when I couldn't see the light at the end of the tunnel and felt like just giving up. I've learned that no matter how bad your circumstances are life does go on. If you keep the faith, it will only get better. There are many lessons learned; however, I will select just a few poignant lessons to share in this chapter.

LESSON #1: HOLD ONTO YOUR FAITH

My dear father held on to his faith. He didn't let go of it while facing life's trials. He believed in God to carry him through the storm. I learned lots of things from my father and believing in God of the Holy Bible was one of them. I learned never to give up and to look at an obstacle as a detour instead of as a roadblock. Often the enemy has hit me with problems that have brought me to my knees and flooded my face with tears. Yet, I refused to give up, even when the pressure was on.

What has kept me is God's unchanging Word. I pray and keep God's Word in my mind and in my heart. I read my Bible daily and speak the scriptures aloud. I attend church hearing the Word preached to me by my pastor. When I listen to my pastor, I feel as if he's talking directly to me, which is a positive indicator that I am on the right track. I write down his sermons as inspiration for the week. My saying is, *If you pray, don't worry. If you worry, don't pray. Don't do both. It's a waste of time and energy to do both.*

I know from experience that you got to believe that the Good Lord knows what He's doing. When things happen, you need to ask yourself, "What is the Lord trying to teach me?" Am I listening or am I so caught up in this world and all its enticements that I have blocked out God's voice? According to John 10:27 (KJV), *"My sheep hear my voice, and I know them, and they follow me,"* and *"So faith comes from hearing, and hearing through the word of Christ,"* Romans 10:17 (ESV). In both Bible verses we learn that we need to listen to God's voice as He will direct our paths.

In the Bible the Lord had decided to destroy the earth. Noah was instructed by God to build an ark and fill it with two of every sort of living thing. Noah continued to listen and follow the Lord's instructions even when people mocked and ridiculed him. When God gives you a mission, even though you can't see through it, you must keep doing it. First you have to listen, and then you must be in the mindset of what is His plan, not what is "my plan." God's not doing anything to you, but He's doing it for you.

I'm an A-type of personality. I am very organized. Being a professor, the first day of class, I have everything in order. I do not take kindly to delays and I try to do more than one thing at a time. I've been this way as far as I can remember. If it wasn't for my faith in God, I'd probably have a nervous breakdown. I don't know what the end is going to be, but I know there is a reason for everything. The Bible teaches us that, *It rains on the just as well as on the unjust,* Matthew 5:45 (NIV). The reason is that the Lord wants to know if we will love Him and have faith in Him during the good times as well as the bad times.

LESSON #2: TELL PEOPLE HOW MUCH YOU APPRECIATE THEM WHILE THEY'RE LIVING

One day someone will call my name, be it my daughters, granddaughters, or even one of my students and I won't answer them. I will be at rest dressed up in my casket. I know this part may be a little startling to read, but one day you will die or someone you love, and respect will no longer be in your presence. Although I try to be the type of person that tells people that I love them and appreciate them while they're breathing, there are a few people I've missed.

One of them is Mrs. Brown, my elementary school teacher. If I could get inside a time machine and travel back to that small two-room schoolhouse, I'd tell her how big of an influence she had on me. I would hug her and kiss her. I'd write a letter like one of my students had written me and explained how she was like a mother to me. That everything she had taught me and the kind words she said to me made a positive impact on my life. Those kind words would be her flowers.

LESSON #3: LEARN TO STAY POSITIVE

When I wasn't teaching a class, I would go ballroom dancing. I took dance classes at the Arthur Murray International Dance Studio, a renowned dance studio that teaches dance all over the country. I love the art of dancing. I love releasing energy, moving my body to the music. Unlike just dancing with friends and family, ballroom dance is much more than just another form of dance. Ballroom dancing takes skills and discipline.

There are two main types of ballroom dance. The first is called the Smooth Style dance and the other is called Rhythm dancing. My instructor, a wonderful and brilliant dancer, taught my class that Smooth Style was flowing dances that move around the entire floor in a counter-clockwise fashion. We would partner up and perform dances called the foxtrot, waltz, tango, and Viennese waltz. Some of the rhythm dances were cha cha, Salsa, and quickstep. I enjoyed dancing and consider ballroom dancing a sport.

During a point in my life when I was going through the difficulties of life, I told myself you can stay in the bed and let depression take over or you can get out of bed and put one foot before the other and carry on. Psychologists at the University of Pennsylvania conducted a study and learned people who experience positive emotions broaden their minds and are more resilient to adversity and achieve more. They bounce back from setbacks more quickly and connect better with others. Ballroom dancing and spending time with the people I love always does it for me.

LESSON #4: STOP HOLDING GRUDGES

I held a grudge against my stepmother for years and it didn't do me any good. I missed out on quality time with her, and I must live with that for the rest of my life. Holding grudges only makes things worse, research discovered. You can't blossom in life when you've focused on the negative. At the end of every storm there is light. We must search for the light and ask God to guide us.

When you allow anger to define you, it affects other parts of your life. You can't enjoy the present, because you're still hanging on to the past. Forgiving isn't easy, but it's a thing you must learn how to do and how to do well. Holding on to the grudges not only affects your personality, holding on to grudges can affect your wellbeing. There are plenty of people who have died of heart attacks, carrying grudges from over ten to fifty years old. Let go and let God handle it. Doesn't the Bible teach us to forgive?

LESSON #5: ENJOY THE FRUITS OF YOUR LABOR

Live in the Moment and Share Your Good Will and Good Deeds with Others

As I mentioned earlier, I'm a type A personality. I read somewhere that people with this type of personality strive toward goals without feeling a sense of joy in their efforts or accomplishments. That sounded like me before I put God first in my life. I've learned to slow down and enjoy life. I advise people to take a moment to enjoy the fruits of their labor. Again, take a moment from your daily routine to look around and admire the beauty of nature, to relax your body, to enjoy the people in your life and to be happy and content.

When you learn to sit back and reflect on life's little pleasures, you are truly living. Life can be so chaotic at times, causing us to miss out on the things that truly matter. We find ourselves complaining about our circumstances or becoming jealous of those whom we think lives are perfect. Believe me no one has a perfect life and are happy all the time. Everyone has struggles, even millionaires and billionaires. They may not have to worry about how to keep the lights on, but they do have other things about which to worry. Some may miss the purpose of why they exist and may find it in drinking or drugs.

LESSON #6: BEAUTY AND THE POWER OF LOVE

Helping disadvantaged children over the years, I've learned that the power of love helps heal past hurts. That's why I make sure to give them lots of hugs and love. The beauty of love is endless. I encourage everyone to go out and find three people to whom they can give praises three times a day. It will not only help them, but also it will help you.

Over the years, I've received numerous plaques, proclamations, certificates, and awards for my work with foster children, community service, and Coppin State University and of course Aunt Hattie's Place. I am a regular on Comcast, CNN Newsmaker, other TV shows, WOLB Internet Radio and frequent newspaper stories about Aunt Hattie's Place and the successes of my foster boys. I'm grateful for all the recognition, but it's not my doing. It's one hundred percent God.

The Lord set the vision for Aunt Hattie's Place. I still have faith that the Lord's Will is still being done—even if I don't understand why and can't see it right now. Frankly, the closing of the third boys group home in Sandy Spring has allowed me the time to reflect on life and write this book. I see it as a faith journey and what the Lord has in store for me. I have read many Bible verses about faith. They have sustained me and have given me the strength I need to stay positive.

When life hands you a lemon, you make lemonade. When there are disappointments in your life, rather than become bitter, depressed and develop a defeatism attitude, stay positive and start another project to use that energy. For example, start training for a race, get on a weight loss program, take up ballroom dancing or Zumba, or commit to some other positive enhancement activity.

Other Little Lessons Learned by Which I Try to Live Daily
- Never give up when life gives you challenges. Rather look at them as bumps in the road or just detours.
- Faith takes less energy than doubt and anger; therefore, don't waste your energy worrying and being angry.
- Family love is not specific to just DNA family members. Any caring and loving person can be like family.
- Happiness doesn't have a dollar sign attached to it. Happiness is a feeling akin to pleasant memories of special people, places and situations in the past, present and the anticipated future.
- Life is what you make it. We must make the most of whatever time we have here on earth rather than living in the past while we are in the present and thinking the future won't be any better than our present.
- However, and in whatever way we think about life, it will become our truth. Is your glass "half full" or "half empty"? Look at life with a new perspective this year! Be optimistic.

Do remember to Keep God First.

Thank-You Letters from My Daughters and Son

A LETTER FROM CHERYL (*Younger Daughter, an Attorney*)

Dearest Mom,

The best way for me to start this letter is to simply say THANK YOU! Thank you for being the type of mother that you have been and are to me, the type of mother who leads by example; who pushes me to exceed even my own expectations; who exemplifies the scripture that says faith without work is dead; who is an advocate of the underdog; who is generous with her time, talent and treasure; who is supportive even when you may not agree with my decisions; who ensured that my sister and I were raised to be well-rounded ladies who believed we could actually become a doctor and a lawyer and not just marry one; and who has become my role model and friend!

Your heart for community service and strong work ethic has greatly impacted my life not just when I worked for you at Aunt Hattie's Place, Inc. for six years, but throughout my career. You have taught me to care about those less fortunate and to respect everyone the same regardless of their socio-economic status. You taught me that relationships are everything and that being kind to people will carry me much farther in life. There are so many things that you have done to make me into the person that I am today! From piano lessons to the ballet, tap, Scottish country dance lessons; to encouraging me to go to law school; from hiring me as the Executive Director of Aunt Hattie's Place at 24 years old, and fresh out of law school; to sending me to Harvard Business School to attend their executive education course in Strategic Perspectives in Nonprofit Management; to ensuring that at a young age and early in my career that I went through the venerable Greater Baltimore Committee's Leadership Program, The Leadership Maryland, the Associate Black Charities Leadership and the Harry and Jeanette Weinberg Nonprofit Executive Directors Fellowship Program. All of these things have impacted my life tremendously!

Words alone can't express how proud I am to call you Mom or convey the deep love, appreciation and respect that I have for you! I wish you nothing but success on this book! You have many jewels and life lessons to share with the world!

Love you,
Your baby girl, Cheryl

~

A LETTER FROM CHARRELL (*Older Daughter, a Physician*)

Letter to My Mother, Dr. Hattie N. Washington

My mother has given so much to my sister and me. I can't begin to tell you how blessed and fortunate I feel to have an incredible, beautiful, God-fearing mother like Hattie Washington. I can only hope to emulate some of these same qualities for my own two daughters. When I was a child, she attended all our school plays/performances and PTA meetings, even after a long day of teaching.

There were times when I wasn't the best child. She not only disciplined me with her hands, but with her words of wisdom. She always said the right things and sacrificed her time for us. I thank her for the endless sacrifices she made in order to give my sister and me a better life than she had growing up. She believed in my dreams of becoming a physician. And, she encouraged me to stay in medical school even when I wanted to give up.

For all of this, I say thank you! To you I say: Kiss and hug your mother; whether she is your birth mother or a woman who has loved you as her own. As the old saying goes, "Give your mother her flowers while she is living." And thank her for just being Mom.

Charrell Washington Thomas, M.D.

~

A TRIBUTE FOR A LIFE CHANGED

by Wayne Saunders

The following is an excerpt from a letter written by Wayne Saunders, foster son of Dr. Hattie N. Washington, as a tribute to his "Mom" and the profound change she has made in his life.

~

While all of the other foster boys call my mom "Aunt Hattie," I call her "Mom," because I feel like I was adopted into her family and lived in her personal home—not the boys' group home. When she officially opened a group home in 1997, I was in the 10th grade and was happy that she loved me enough to keep me in her personal home so I could finish the high school I was attending at the time.

As the first person in my family to graduate from college and to now be employed in the IT field, you need to understand why I am so appreciative for the impact, influence and inspiration this phenomenal woman has had in my life. My older brother and I came into foster care when I was eleven years old, because my birth mom was addicted to drugs. We were placed in two different group homes. I was blessed to be placed with Dr. Washington, who at the time was the Assistant Superintendent of Baltimore City Schools. I had been in and out of different schools, because of my unstable home situation. Unfortunately, my brother never did go to college; however, my "Mom" promoted education and exposed me to numerous mentors, cultural enrichment, recreational and spiritual activities, which have led me to become the person that I am today.

Despite my circumstances, my mom raised me to always give back and try to help someone else as she helped me. She said to me early on, when she took me in her home when I was eleven years old, that she was going to give me an opportunity to make something of myself, but it was going to be up to me to make it happen. In addition, she constantly told me over and over that there is a reason for everything and not to be angry with by birth mom or other relatives who could not take me to live with them. I later understood what she meant when I walked across the stage at my college graduation.

My mom is my role model. She has been an excellent example for me to emulate as well as her two daughters—my (foster) sisters—one a physician and the other an attorney. Therefore, my goal is to always live up to the high expectations she has always instilled in me and to give back to the community. If I can influence one person (especially other foster males) to make something of themselves, I will.

~

Interviews

Aunt Hattie
Cheryl Washington
Reverend Samuel Williams, Jr.
Robert "Bob" Hamlin
Rebecca "Beck" Lee
†Reverend J. Samuel Williams, Jr.
†Robert "Bob" Hamlin
†Joy Cabarrus Speakes
†Edwilda Allen

---

†Interviews of the original strikers of the R. R. Moton High School Strike in 1951 were held at the Moton Museum, 711 Griffin Blvd. Farmville, VA 23901.
–Narrative Interviews of Joy Cabarrus Speakes and Elwilda Allen, original strikers of the R. R. Moton High School in 1951 that was the catalyst for the historic landmark case of *Brown v. Board of Education.*
–Extensive Interviews with Reverend J. Samuel Williams, Jr., Pastor of the Levi Baptist Church in Green Bay, Virginia in Prince Edward County and Robert ("Bob") Hamlin, Docent who served as a guide to the R. R. Moton Museum collections of that historic era). Reverend Williams and Bob Hamlin were also part of the original Strike of 1951 and were affected by the school closing.

THE HOUSE OF RUTH—Assisting Families Victimized by Domestic Violence

www.houseofruthinc.org
House of Ruth
P.O. Box 459
Claremont, CA 91711
Phone: 909-623-4364
Fax: 909-629-9581
24-Hour Crisis Hotline: (877) 988-5559

RESOURCE LIST FOR THE SIGNIFICANCE OF R. R. MOTON MUSEUM IN PRINCE EDWARD COUNTY, VIRGINIA

These resources can be used to educate readers about the significance of this area and the impact it had leading up to the landmark case *Brown v. Board of Education*. Please visit the Moton Museum in Farmville, Virginia, and the website: www.motonmuseum.org. This will also assist with the funding of the museum while sharing the history of this community abroad.

Books
1. *They Closed Their Schools*, by Bob Smith.
2. *The Moton School Story: Children of Courage*, text by Larissa Smith Ferguson, Ph.D.
3. *Bound for Freedom*, by Neil Sullivan.
4. *Browns Battleground*, by Jill Ogline Titus.
5. *You Need a Schoolhouse*, by Stephanie Deutsch.
6. *The Girl from the Tarpaper School: Barbara Johns and the Advent of the Civil Rights Movement*, by Teri Kanefield;
7. *Students on Strike, A Memoir of John A. Stokes*, with LolaWolfe Ph.D.
8. *Exilic Existence*, by Rev. J. Samuel Williams Jr.
9. *Educated in Spite Of: A Promise Kept*, by Dorothy L. Holcomb;

DVDs
1. *Strike: A Call to Action: The Dramatic Story of the 1951 Student Strike*
2. *Farmville: An American Story* (one-of-a-kind Moton item, must get on site of the Moton Museum in Farmville, VA)
3. *Mr. Stokes' Mission: A Story about Education and Equality*
4. *The Vernon Johns Story: The Road to Freedom.*

Links
1. www.motonmuseum.org
2. http://www.encyclopediavirginia.org/search?type=article&keywords= Barbara+Johns
3. http://www.encyclopediavirginia.org/Moton_School_Strike_and_Prince_Edward_County_ School_Closings
4. http://www.encyclopediavirginia.org/Hill_Oliver_W_1907–2007
5. http://www.encyclopediavirginia.org/Massive_Resistance
6. http://www.encyclopediavirginia.org/media_player?mets_filename=evm00001062mets.xml
7. http://www.encyclopediavirginia.org/Farmville_Protests_of_1963
8. http://www.pbs.org/wnet/jimcrow/stories_people_johns.html
9. http://www.archives.gov/education/lessons/davis-case/
10. http://www.lva.virginia.gov/exhibits/brown/decision.htm
11. http://www.neh.gov/humanities/2013/septemberoctober/feature/massive-resistance-in-small-town
12. http://americanhistory.si.edu/brown/history/4-five/farmville-virginia-1.html

OTHER ORGANIZATIONS THAT SUPPORT CHILDREN AND POSITIVE CHANGE

National Council For Negro Women, www.ncnw.org
Today, the National Council of Negro Women, Inc. (NCNW) is a council of 39 affiliated national African American women's organizations and over 240 sections, connecting nearly 4 million women worldwide. The Mission of the NCNW is to lead, develop and advocate for women of African descent as they support their families and communities. We fulfill our mission through research, advocacy and national and community-based health, education and economic empowerment services and programs in the United States and Africa. Through section and affiliate volunteers in 34 states, NCNW addresses local needs while impacting communities nationwide. For more information and to join, visit website: www.ncnw.org

The Children Defense Fund (CDF)
The CDF is an American child advocacy and research group, founded in 1973 by Marian Wright Edelman. Its motto, Leave No Child Behind, reflects its mission to advocate on behalf of children. The organization is leading our nation to ensure a level playing field for all children supported by private donations. For more information about CDF, visit their website: http://www.childrensdefense.org/25 E. St. NW, Washington, DC

Black Women For Positive Change (BW4PC)
Bkwomen4Poschange@gmail.com
http://www.blackwomenforpositivechange.org/
Black Women for Positive Change is a national policy-focused network, organized in 2013, has two primary goals: (1) To positively contribute to ideas and methods that can strengthen and expand the American Middle/Working class, with an emphasis on the African

American community; and (2) To Change the Culture of Violence in America. For more information, visit their website: **http://www.blackwomenforpositivechange.org/**

Success

To laugh often and much;
to win the respect of intelligent people and the affection of children;
to earn the appreciation of honest critics and
endure the betrayal of false friends;
to appreciate beauty;
to find the beauty in others;
to leave the world a bit better whether by a healthy child,
a garden patch, or a redeemed social condition;
to know that one life has breathed easier because you lived here.
This is to have succeeded."

– RALPH WALDO EMERSON

Special Recognition from the Author

I would like to give a special recognition to the following people: Thank you to Lorenzo Goganious, his wife, Bettie, his sister, Barbara and his entire family. They have offered prayers, encouragement and a tranquil setting to write the first book (memoir) as well as this revised updated edition.

Thank you to my sisters Jean, Terrie, Sheila (husband, Walter), Edna, Eula and my brothers, Bishop Dr. Samuel Neal, III, Larry Lee and Arnold Neal; William Johns (who read the first book and sent in several comments of accolades for the book), all other relatives and extended members, and all of my Mentor Mothers and Fathers who have influenced my life, including those who are not listed in this memoir.

Thank you to my Village Supporters who continue to encourage me, offer prayers and support: Renee Robinson, Wilma Dean, Malcolm Riley, Jean Hundley, Reverend Samuel Neal, III, Terrie Waddell, Larry Lee, Sheila and Walter Clark, Arnold Neal, Barbara and Ike Munden, Lorenzo and Miriam Goganious, III (LG); Keith and Ingrid Goganious, Jackie Goganious, Charlie Ella Clark, Phyllis and Anthony Freeman, Ethel Mitchell, and Eric Waddy.

Thank you to Reverend Dr. Haywood A. Robinson, III and The People's Community Baptist Church (TPCBC), and The Coalition of Faith-Based Institutions, Reverend Dr. Henry P. Davis, III and The First Baptist Church of Highland Park.

Thank you to my Coppin State University Family: Dr. Mortimer Neufville, Dr. Sadie Gregory, Dr. James Takona and CASE Faculty and Staff, especially my friends, colleague and staff of the School of Education (SOE), and my Teaching and Learning Department: Dr.

Yi Huang, Marjorie Miles, Jackie Williams, Daniel Joseph, Glynis Barber, Delores Harvey, Mable Murray, Jean Ragin, Johnnie Brinson, Jermaine Ellerbe, Thomas James, Gerri Bohana, Robert Eccles, Alexandria Ryce, Daphanie Roseborough, Ashley McLeod and much appreciation to Arlene Samuel, Karen Lewis, Veronica Mack, Victoria Johnson and Deborah Stone, Doug Dalzell and Staff, Andrew Brezinsky, Eunice Fall, Tara Turner, Tiffany Jones, Dr. Mary Wanza, Dr. Mary Owens, Dr. Judith Wilner, Dr. Washington's Former Students, Tamaria Price, Florence Onyekaonwu, Wendy Bozel.

Thank you to The Robert Russa Moton Museum and The Farmville Virginia Connection: Sherre Atkins, Brenda Richards, Shirley Eanes; Joy Cabarrus Speakes and Edwilda Allen (original strikers of the R. R. Moton High School in 1951 for their Interviews), Robert Hamlin, Docent of Moton Museum; Reverend J. Samuel Williams, Jr., Pastor and Congregation of Levi Baptist Church in Green Bay, VA; Rebecca "Beck" Lee Randolph (Memory Lane Tour Guide), Patricia Lee Adams, and Shirley Reed Ray, Reverend Barbara Reed, Dora Reed, Estelle McCormick, Ralph Stokes, Juanita McCormick, Kea Taylor of Imagine Photography (www.imaginephotography.com), and Edmund Warthen of Warthen Photos (www.dwarthenphoto.com).

Thank you to my Facebook, LinkedIn friends, as well as friends of my daughters and son.

Special Note
If I omitted to thank anyone,
please chalk it up to my head,
not my heart.
Thank you one and all.
Much Love and God Bless.
Hattie

HE WHO KNOWS

"He who knows, but knows not How to express what he knows;
will become less sure, as time elapses,
and may even wonder
IF
he ever knew at first."

– DR. HATTIE N. WASHINGTON

RECIPE FOR A HAPPY LIFE

"A Pinch of Prayer for A Purpose;
A Dash of Dedication to A Cause;
A Handful of Hugs for The Heart;
A Spoonful of Smiles for The Soul;
And A Forkful of Faith for God's Favor.

Marinade them all Together with Patience and
Persistence; Bake Until Golden, and
Serve With TLC—Tender Loving Care."

– AUNT HATTIE (DR. HATTIE N. WASHINGTON)

Another Book by Dr. Hattie N. Washington

AUNT HATTIE'S SOUTHERN COMFORT FOOD FAVORITES

Aunt Hattie Enjoying One of Her Favorite Pastime Activities: Cooking Southern Cuisine

ABOUT THE AUTHOR: Dr. Washington's education includes a Bachelor of Science Degree in Elementary Education with a minor in Special Education from Norfolk State University; a Master's Degree in Counseling Psychology from Ball State University (Athens, Greece Overseas Program); and a Doctorate in Curriculum and Instruction from the University of Maryland College Park. She has engaged in further post-graduate study in Multicultural Education and Special Education at Glasgow University in Scotland, UK (on a Rotary International Fellowship); and Executive Management at Harvard University in Boston; and then Institutional Accountability in Higher Education at Oxford University in London, England. She taught for years in the United States, in Greece, and Scotland, UK.

Dr. Washington was the first female Vice President of Coppin State University (CSU). Prior to CSU, she was Assistant Superintendent of Baltimore City Public Schools (BCPS) where the vision of Aunt Hattie's Place, a home for foster boys, originated. And, prior to

BCPS, she was Program Specialist for the Maryland State Department of Education (MSDE). She has received numerous awards, plaques, citations and other recognitions for her work with Aunt Hattie's Place, CSU, foster children, and community organizations. Just a few include: Top 100 Minority Business Entrepreneurial of the Year (2009 and 2012), and the Maryland Women's Commission 2018 Hall of Fame Award, honoring five outstanding women who exemplify a "Legacy of Leadership, Service and Excellence."

Dr. Washington is a devoted mother of two accomplished daughters (a physician and an attorney), proud grandmother of two precious granddaughters, and foster mother to over one hundred foster boys over a 22-year period.

She resides in Maryland, where she enjoys spending her leisure time reading, writing, motivational speaking, community service ("giving back"), traveling, ballroom dancing, cooking Southern cuisine, learning to play the piano, and just spending time with family and friends.

To learn more about Dr. Washington's book *Driven to Succeed: An Inspirational Memoir of Lessons Learned through Faith, Family, and Favor,* and her other published book, *Aunt Hattie's Cookbook: Southern Comfort Food Favorites,* please contact her directly at: drhattie@washingtonpublishingenterprises.com; and/ or visit her website at: www.drhnwashington.com.

Thank You for Reading!

Dear Reader,

Thank you for reading *DRIVEN TO SUCCEED: An Inspirational Memoir of Lessons Learned Through Faith, Family and Favor*. I trust that you enjoyed this labor-of-love book.

As an author, I love feedback. Your comments about by down-home cooking and recipes straight from the gardens, orchards, barnyard and pasture generated numerous requests to write a cookbook. Thus, the birth of an unintended cookbook: *Aunt Hattie's Cookbook: Southern Comfort Food Favorites*.

So, keep telling me what you liked. I would love to hear from you. You can write me at info@drhnwashington.com and visit me on my website at: www.drhnwashington.com (My *DRIVEN TO SUCCEED* book is available in paperback, hardcover, e-book, has been translated into Spanish, and coming soon, an audio book).

If you are so inclined after reading one of my books, I'd love a written review sent to my author's page on Amazon.com.

Thanks again for reading my book and providing me with feedback.

In gratitude,
Hattie Washington

www.ingramcontent.com/pod-product-compliance
Lightning Source LLC
Chambersburg PA
CBHW030051100526
44591CB00008B/103